D0058206

O. J. in the Morning,
G&T at Night

—

Also by A. E. Hotchner

O. J. in the Morning, G&T at Night

—

*Spirited Dispatches on Aging
with Joie de Vivre*

A. E. Hotchner

St. Martin's Press

New York

www.stmartins.com

Design by Kathryn Parise

ISBN 978-1-250-02821-1 (hardcover)
ISBN 978-1-250-02820-4 (e-book)

First Edition: February 2013

10 9 8 7 6 5 4 3 2 1

Dedicated to my mother and father,
who prospered into their eighties, and to my brother,
who touched ninety

Contents

HALCYON DAYS

Not from successful love alone,
Nor wealth, nor honor'd middle age, nor victories of
  politics or war;
But as life wanes, and all the turbulent passions calm,
As gorgeous, vapory, silent hues cover the evening sky,
As softness, fullness, rest, suffuse the frame, like fresher,
  balmier air,
As the days take on a mellower light, and the apple
  at last hangs really finish'd and indolent-ripe on
  the tree,
Then for the teeming quietest, happiest days of all!
The brooding and blissful halcyon days!

  —Walt Whitman, at seventy

O. J. in the Morning,
G&T at Night

—

We are all happier in many ways when we are old than when we were young. The young sow wild oats. The old grow sage.

—Winston Churchill

The Evening News Is Bad
for Your Health

~

Last year, I stopped watching the evening news when it dawned on me that it was virtually a medicine cabinet sponsored by pharmaceuticals with their eyes on the aging viewers. Woven around Brian, Diane, and Scott were identical commercials promoting cures for a conglomerate of human ills, ranging from erectile dysfunction to overactive bladders. Night after night, a self-propelled gurney follows a healthy-looking individual who is unaware that, as shown in a graphic insert, his veins are stockpiling corpuscles that spell doom. And then there's the guy in a ballpark, watching a game with his buddies, who has to dash for the lavatory, thereby missing the walk-off home run in the last of the ninth. The next newscast, he's in a rowboat fishing with those buddies when the selfsame urge to go overwhelms him and they have to go to shore to accommodate him. If only he had taken the sponsor's pill, we are told, his friendly-induced bladder would not have interrupted the fishing. His other option, of course, would have been to simply piss over the side.

I have no idea what defines "erectile dysfunction." Totally inoperative? Half willing? Only operative under specific conditions? Popping off too soon? Takes forever? Only functions once a month? One thing is sure: There is fierce competition on the evening news for control of the American penis. Viagra, Cialis, and Levitra are the competitors, with Cialis outspending its rivals with a saturation of dramas that illustrate its slogan, intoned by a mellifluous male voice: *You can be ready!* This readiness is a daily Cialis or the thirty-six-hour jumbo that can put out an untold number of female sexual fires during that period. The only sobering caveat is that if any erection lasts longer than four hours, the erectionee should immediately seek help from his doctor (presumably the M.D. who prescribed it in the first place) or from the emergency room. Of course, in the waiting room vestiges of his erection will be on display, which may be embarrassing or prideful depending on the bearer's personality.

To illustrate its You Can Be Ready alert (variously pronounced You *Can* Be Ready and You Can Be *Ready*), Cialis presents a series of unlikely events: a couple handling a load of wash, the basket of dirty clothes between them, their eyes lock, music soars, a waterfall inundates the laundry room, the walls collapse morphing into a super-lush garden,

2

running stream, and the couple, instantly rid of their clothes basket, are mooning on the bank, the "event" presumably consummated outside our view. Another Cialis moment occurs in a kitchen where the man is bringing a bowl filled with red peppers to a woman who is standing at the sink. As he hands her the bowl of peppers, she gets a dreamy look, his eyes widen, and quicker than you can say "Call the plumber!" water overflows from the sink, cascading onto the floor, creating a flood that washes the couple out the door and into a rendezvous nook somewhere in the tropics, where they are seated at an elegant table overlooking the sea while they hold hands and enjoy their post-copulated state.

Another of these priceless Cialis moments puts a woman on a ladder, painting a living room wall, a man on the carpet below her. The woman comes down the ladder, hands him her paintbrush, the man takes one look at her, discards the paintbrush, and they start politely dancing as the room overflows with a torrent of watery paint that gushes them into a lush, tropical garden where they cozy up on a fern-laden bank while that mellifluous voice sings Cialis's praises. Each of these universal moments ends with the man and woman naked, occupying adjoining bathtubs on an ocean's shore, looking out to sea, their backs to us. Makes one wonder why they are not in just one tub if Cialis really hit the mark.

Given the average age of the evening news' core audience,

I don't think a basket of dirty clothes or a bucket of peppers or a woman exuding Eau de Turpentine resonates, but then again Cialis might ignite the imagination of a seventy-year-old to believe that he could stud some of the more desirable assisted-living ladies over a thirty-six-hour spree. Realistically, gentlemen of the "mature" group could possibly wind up in the emergency room or in the morgue suffering from the aftereffects of frivolous fornication.

Of course, if the Cialis guy in the kitchen with the peppers was a Viagra man, he would have had to sit around in the kitchen, with his woman panting, and wait an hour "before the event" for the Viagra to run up his sail. On the other hand, how many men encounter sexual combustion over a bucket of peppers? Also, how many men wind up in the emergency ward? The same couple that lit such a sexual bonfire over their encounter in front of that Maytag conclude their idyllic escapade by looking straight at the camera and warning everyone of all the dire reactions they may have if they take the Cialis they have just taken, everything from falling arches to going deaf, dumb, and blind.

At the rate Cialis is spending for commercials across the television spectrum virtually every night, to justify such a hefty expenditure it would suggest that half the men in America have penises that are as dysfunctional as the stock market.

It is of note that both Cialis and Viagra urge their viewers to "see our ad in *Golf Digest*," thereby identifying golfers as prime targets for the erectile dysfunction business. Makes one wonder if a steady diet of thirty-six-hour Cialis may have contributed to Tiger Woods's undoing.

Furthermore, since all these penis enhancers require a doctor's prescription, it looks like erectile dysfunction may be the only medical condition for which a doctor will write a prescription without an examination. Tell your doctor you've got a bad cough and you'd like a prescription for penicillin, you won't get it unless he examines you. Same applies to your request for digitalis for your palpitations, or insulin because you suspect you have diabetes. But what examination does a doctor conduct to determine if a patient, requesting Cialis or Viagra, has erectile dysfunction?

I asked my doctor about that and he acknowledged that in writing prescriptions for erectile dysfunction he simply had to take his patient's word for it—if he was physically qualified for such sexual activity. "But I do impose one restraint. When I first wrote these prescriptions, I was bombarded with phone calls from my patients' outraged wives who blamed me for the preposterous increase in their husbands' sexual desires. Now when I write these prescriptions, I make my patients promise not to tell their wives about the prescriptions I wrote for them."

One more thing about Cialis: Since it provides continual hours of instant fornication, what has happened to foreplay? Seniors' extended foreplay was an ingredient of their sex lives, but now? Without giving a thought to his unprepared partner, the Cialis male can hop right to it (*You can be ready!*), carefree except for the ominous warning that after four hours of Cialising he has to be deerectionized probably by the physician who wrote the prescription that got him into this pickle.

Many of the supplicant drug companies on the evening news broadcast similar caveats about the possible calamitous effects of their products. Chantix, for example, a prescription medicine designed to help smokers stop, warns users that if they are obsessing about committing suicide or making actual attempts to commit suicide, or fall into deep depressions, suffer from panic attacks, turn angry and violent, have hallucinations, paranoia or dangerous impulses, they should immediately get to their doctor. Of course, if they are about to commit suicide, or battling paranoia, they are not about to drop everything and give doc a call. I can't picture this distraught person putting aside his gun or closing the fifteenth-story window he has been standing in front of, itching to jump, or capping the bottle of sleeping pills in his hand and waiting patiently for his doctor to call him back with some encouraging words.

Other prescription elixirs also warn of possible side effects, likely on advice of their lawyers: sudden hair loss, teetering teeth, bleeding bowels, loss of vision, suffocating neck pressure, severe diarrhea, bloody urine, unbearable cramps, acute chest pains, loss of hearing, to name a few.

Most of the fake doctors who write these fake prescriptions for fake patients come from casting agencies. It is an exception when a bona fide physician appears in one of the medical sketches. Probably because it's not easy finding authentic M.D.s who are camera ready, able to memorize lines, and willing to sully their reputations by getting paid to playact their profession. Perhaps medical schools could include a course in acting, run by the Actors Studio, so that needy doctors could augment their incomes. That would entice agents to look for photogenic docs who could hit camera marks, act dignified, and speak in an authoritative manner. None of the doctors I know come readily to mind.

Getting back to that self-propelled gurney that is in ominous motion night after night on the trail of a variety of potential victims—a golfer, a night watchman, a businessman—each episode with a happy ending: The potential victim goes straight to his doctor as the gurney peals off at the doctor's door. The distinguished doctor, replete with white jacket and a stethoscope coiled around his neck, receives the night watchman in his office. In very small letters at the bottom of the screen there appears: "Doctor and patient dramatization." This actor-cum-doctor, unwinds the stethoscope from his neck and tepidly aims it at the watchman's chest that is fully clothed; the doc nods knowingly and goes to his desk to write a prescription that will assuredly unblock the patient's arteries. Over the years I have had countless encounters with doctors stethoscoping my chest and back, but not once without being required to bare my chest and submit to multiple pokes of the stethoscope. This bogus nightly news doctor now writes a prescription with the medication's name, PLAVIX, in large block letters that he underlines. I have never received a prescription that was even remotely legible nor was the commercial name of the product. If this legibility keeps up, doctors' universal reputation for undecipherable prescriptions is going to be given a good name.

If you are as susceptible to autosuggestion as I am, then you, too, have been victimized by the knavery of the evening news' repetitions. For example Flomax, which sponsored the guy who rushes to the pissoir in the last of the ninth, capped that drama with a nightly pissing menu: Difficulty starting the flow? Going too often? Embarrassing leaks? Starting and stopping? Weak stream? Difficulty emptying? I realized how brain-washed I had become when I was at a urinal one evening during a Philharmonic intermission, and I suddenly became aware of the intensity of the stream flowing into the urinal next to me, clearly several decibels louder than my stream. There flashed across my eyes: WEAK STREAM. Although we had unzipped our flows at the same time, my neighbor topped off way before I did. It would have never occurred to me that I had a weak stream had Flomax not posted it on its menu. But then, I brooded, what constitutes "weak"? Perhaps urinals could have built-in radars like those used to measure the velocity of baseballs.

Along with the automatic flush, the urinal would display a number, 1–10, 1 being the weakest. That way you'd know where your stream stood—a solid 8, say, might make you feel pretty macho. Friend calls, says how's it going? I'd say, oh, I hit 7 yesterday. How about you? I was a solid 9 this morning. Taking Flomax? Yeah.

It was at that point last year, I stopped watching the evening news.

Time and tide wait for no man, but time always stands still for a woman of thirty.

—ROBERT FROST

You Can Drown in the Fountain of Youth

Although we expend considerable money and effort trying to postpone the inevitable, the hard, cold universal fact is that there is no known way to avoid stockpiling our advancing years with its telltale evidence. We can slice years off our ages by doctoring our passports and our drivers' licenses, but our hands, legs, faces, necks, and hair give us away. We insist on trying to cover up the obvious, however, which is like insisting, with unending buckets of quarters, that one can conquer the slots at Caesars Palace and Foxwoods.

The many people I know who have tried to staunch the trickle of aging. have started by trying to obliterate those baggy eyes, crows' feet, frown lines, heavy lids, and escalating wrinkles that mock them in the bathroom mirror. And the neck, with its incipient double chin and turkey waddle enters the picture. No matter how skilled and costly the doctors are, their handiwork can be spotted: the wide-open, unblinking eyes, the motionless forehead, the crooked smile. There aren't many facelifts that truly lift the face. It was Anne de Lenclos who lamented, "If God had to give a woman wrinkles, He might at least have put them on the soles of her feet."

I knew Joan Rivers long before her makeover by the dermatological wizards whose expensive labors produced an expanse of tightly stretched skin better suited for Bruce Springsteen's drum set. Now when Joan laughs, laughter comes out of her but her mouth doesn't move, which is a phenomenon that can't be easily explained.

Another friend, in his eighties, who owned a string of fashionable men's shops, was very upset by the inroads wrinkles were inflicting on his face. A man of considerable fashion, known for his derby hats, exotic vests, and colorful bow ties, he decided the time had come to obliterate the wrinkle scourge that was upsetting his image. He underwent a full facelift that turned out to be much slower healing and more painful than he had anticipated. I saw him a week after he had been released from the hospital and asked him if he was satisfied with the outcome. "For the most part, yes," he said, "although now when I shave my cheeks are behind my ears."

And then there was the acquaintance who fancied that she would improve her profile if she removed the small, pointed tip of her nose, expecting the procedure to be as quick and easy as her Botox injections. It wasn't. She said she had to sleep in an upright position for a week, and that her nose was very painful, especially when she sneezed. As far as I could tell, her profile looked the same. I didn't tell her that.

Speaking of Botox devotees, I wonder if there is a possibility that the disappearing Botox might be leaching from the irrigated gullies of their faces into their cranial cavities. After all, there is a current scientific investigation into whether prolific cell phone users might be zapping their brains with emanations from those phones that are constantly in their ears. What if the disappearing Botox liquid was headed in the same direction?

When I was writing a book about Doris Day, I discovered that she believed that a person who endures a traditional face-lift with all its chanciness, is much better served by a nonintrusive inner face-lift. "I think the greatest face-lift is a thinking lift," she said. "Our faces reflect what we're thinking, and when we have clouded, negative, bitter thoughts, our faces and our eyes show these things no matter what we do with foundations and eye shadows. When thoughts are positive and loving, a person's entire face relaxes. Down lines go up. Worry lines ease out. The body lifts in spirit. The soul is uplifted. It's the greatest cosmetic of all, and it doesn't cost a cent."

Any discussion of physical aging must, perforce, include hair. As far as the ladies are concerned, how they style and color their hair is really between themselves and their hair-dressers, although an occasional yelp from a husband might possibly be considered, but for the most part he is ignored. Yelps about color, however, are treated a bit more seriously. Solid black, brown with highlights, shades of blonde, letting gray assert itself, usually don't invoke much controversy, but there is one color that does: red. When it is natural, radiantly ruby or garnet, red hair is catnip to whistling males. But not for long. My mother had the most beautiful red hair you can imagine, but when it faded she could not bear to let it go. Over the years she experimented with endless shades of red but none of them truly worked. There were fire engine reds and cardinal reds and orangey reds but they didn't look like they belonged on top of her head. To this day, I think that ladies who have ventured into the red spectrum have suf-fered my mother's fate. The Association of Titian-Haired Beauticians will probably jump me, but having been a noto-rious redhead in my youth I fancy myself a lifelong authority on the subject. I can tell you that a thatch of red on top of a boy's head can be a source of derision and embarrassment, especially when, like me, you have a face peppered with freckles. Hey Red! Hey Rusty! Hey Carrot-top! Norman Rockwell painted the likes of me fishing with my grandpa or posed with a friendly policeman. A grown-up redhead is simply not taken seriously. I don't think any of our presi-dents or vice presidents had red hair. Or captains of indus-try. Or movie heart throbs. Red hair is okay for athletes and comedians but that's about it. Those men cursed with red hair can take solace in the fact that burgeoning gray strands will eventually mute and then obliterate their bloody looks.

But getting back to those women who, like my mother, strive to perpetuate their red hair, fortune awaits whoever produces a truly red hair color, which has been as elusive as the black tulip.

Most men are not much interested in changing the color of their hair, although drugstores do have preparations that will cover up outcroppings of gray. Men are not prone to becoming overnight blonds, redheads, or tinting blue. The pervasive hair concern of the aging male is how to deal with incipient baldness. Should side strands be pulled over the naked crown? How about combing the hair from back to front, a la Napoleon? Or perhaps shaving it all off to create a bald, polished pate like Bruce Willis and Michael Jordan. (I deliberately left out toupees.) None of the choices is very appealing.

Nor is it appealing to watch those in the upper age-brackets trying to imitate the young in a misconceived, pathetic effort to recapture their youth. Cultivating friendships with those who are younger is certainly desirable but in other matters there is a divide that is too wide to be breeched. Every evolving generation has its own vernacular: clothes, styles, clubs, dances, music, bands, performers, and so forth. They are indigenous and attempts to copy them by those far up the age ladder produce ridicule rather than acceptance. It is not a pretty sight when a "mature" gentleman whose generation danced with arms around and cheeks touching, ventures onto a club's dance floor and tries to mimic what is pulsating around him. I have both observed it and painfully experienced it when pulled into the maelstrom by an enthusiastic young lady who afterward bestowed a "good sport" commendation upon me.

But I have found that there are certain simple changes that can make the older set of both sexes feel younger without taking them out of their element. The aftershave balm, the perfume, the cologne you've been using all these years, it's about time to go sniff around an upscale cosmetic counter and find an exciting replacement that will give you an olfactory boost. Those garments that have hung in your closet forever may need a trip to the Goodwill, to be succeeded by a new dress or the first new suit in how long? New clothes may be a superficial contribution but if it makes you preen a bit in front of your mirror, lighten your step, perk up your face, isn't it worth it?

I had been spritzing 4711 as my aftershave for many years until one morning I realized I wasn't aware of its fragrance any more. I made an enjoyable tour sampling the Ralph Lauren, Tommy Hilfiger, Calvin Klein, Tom Ford offerings and settled on Hilfiger, which put a much appreciated snap into my morning ritual, but a whiff of a heady, new fragrance can lead to embarrassing misperceptions. I speak from experience. There was a time, several years ago, when I felt that I had gone stale and I decided to undertake a personal reclamation project, beginning with my wardrobe. It was a period when Indian clothes were coming into vogue. It seemed that there were as many saris in fashion magazines and Madison Avenue show windows as there were in Bombay.

I had just seen a handsome Nehru jacket on display in a Bergdorf Goodman for Men window, and I decided that it would be the proper look for my Pygmalion turn. The jacket had a high collar, embroidered pocket flaps, pearl buttons, and a rose-colored foulard that the sales person said was de rigeur for the Nehru. Also, at the salesman's behest, I purchased a pair of black leather square-toed boots that laced up the side. Good-bye to stuffy old Hotch. The new look made me feel . . . mischievous. I decided to wear my Indian costume that evening to a fifth anniversary party for a young couple I knew. I had even bought a matching Nehru ankle-length topcoat.

I was the only man at the party wearing a Nehru and there were no saris on the ladies. It seemed that the Indian clothing invasion had landed in the high-end stores and magazines but not on the backs of the younger generation. My Nehru faux pas had taught me a lesson: whatever you wear it must look like it *belongs* on your back. My Nehru perhaps belonged on someone's back but not mine. George Clooney would be the Prince of the Ganges, but on me, I looked like an outcast from the Salvation Army.

I should have known that you cannot force clothes on yourself any more than as a writer you can force yourself to write something that is alien to your capabilities. One time, for example, when I received a phone call from Marlene Dietrich who had been a friend for many years, asking me to help her write an article to be entitled, "The Danger When Beauty Fades." Marlene always lived far beyond her means and she had accepted a sizeable advance from *McCall's Magazine* for such an article, spent the advance, but didn't have the time (she was performing in Las Vegas) nor the ability to deliver this article for which *McCall's* was now pressing: either deliver the article (which was six months in arrears), or return the advance, which she didn't have.

She sent me a few disjointed notes she had scribbled on a piece of Sands' stationery, that she thought might fuel my literary endeavor, but I phoned and told her that I was really not equipped to write about that subject. She pleaded: she was broke, couldn't return the advance, please, please give it a try and rescue her.

I went through her scribbles, talked to her on the phone a few times, and I did attempt to write something coherent and interesting but I was wandering around in unfamiliar territory, one version more discouraging than the next. I finally went to see her at her Fifth Avenue apartment (she had concluded her Vegas stint) with my last attempt. I could see from the look on her face that she was reading the manuscript with increasing dismay.

I said, "I'm sorry. I really tried but it's not a subject I could handle."

"I can tell." She lit a cigarette and watched the smoke; the silence was uncomfortable.

"Well, I'd best be going," I said, rising. "I'm sure you'll work something out," a lame comment if ever there was one.

At the door, we said our good-byes, her eyes showing her disappointment in me. "You've both let me down," she said.

"Both?"

"First, Jean Cocteau, and now you—you've both failed me."

"Jean Cocteau tried to write this article for you?"

"Yes, a couple of versions."

I must confess that when I left I was not at all dejected but rather elated to have shared failure with such distinguished company.

I offered my Nehru package, jacket, foulard, boots, and topcoat, to a young man who was assisting me with research. He tried on everything, looked at himself in the mirror, and, thanking me, decided to wear it the following night at his girlfriend's Halloween party.

Grow old with me!
The best is yet to be.
—ROBERT BROWING

O.J. in the Morning,
G&T at Night

———

When I turned seventy-five I was under the illusion that given all the challenges I had faced in my life, I could handle any rough stuff that came my way, like being blind-sided or sucker punched. I believed I was a battle-savvy veteran, equipped to fend off the pesky slings and arrows, duck the custard pies and sharp elbows, anticipate the deceptions and connivances that might come zinging my way.

But as I was about to find out on the day after my seventy-fifth birthday, there is no defense against being thrown a curve when you're least expecting it. The nibbling encroachment of your passing years—the fading biceps, reflexes, knees, rotator cuffs, conspire against you. You freeze, your back leg buckles, you pull away as the curve dives over the plate, and you hear those fatal words: "You're out!"

On the morning of the first day of my seventy-sixth year, my second wife, to whom I had been married for twenty years, came to the breakfast table and, pushing my newspaper aside, said: "I am leaving you."

"Oh," I said naively, "you have an appointment?"

"Yes. With a broker. I'm moving into a sublet."

There had been no preamble to this pronouncement, no dirge of dissatisfaction, no soul-searching confessional, no litany of neglect and abuse, selfishness and niggardliness. Nope, I had my back to the plate when she threw this curve—which landed like a beanball.

Matter of fact, it wasn't much of a marriage. Our interests, our personalities, our friends, our sense of humor (or lack of it), our beliefs, our temperaments, nothing meshed, except for our fondness for our son who was born a year into our marriage. When my two daughters of my previous marriage were young (my first wife died of cancer), I was often away serving the demands of freelance writing. But now, with the security of accomplishment, I intended to stay the course and enjoy the growing years of this splendid little son; unfortunately that meant tolerating my flat marital existence. It may well have also been my wife's motivation.

But now she was cramming the station wagon with all her belongings and, with a wave of her hand, she was disappearing down the driveway. I was conflicted: pleased to see this sham relationship come to an end, but unsure of my footing.

Our son was now in his third year at Brown University, presently on an exchange program in Nepal. I decided to go visit him and break the news about this unexpected fissure on the home front. My wife declared she would go at the same time so as not to give me a leg up on who did what to whom.

It was, without doubt, the most bizarre trip I ever took anywhere. It was Christmastime and the highlight of my three days there was when the Nepalese waiters in the hotel dressed in their version of Santa Claus costumes (looking more like the seven dwarfs), and sang "Jingle Bells" with an incomprehensible Nepalese accent to a tune that sounded like a Gregorian chant.

Our talk with our son was anticlimatic.

"What took you so long?" he said.

Suddenly a bachelor, I now had to invent a reordered existence. I felt it was important to stick to the base of my usual routine: out of bed and start the day on the floor stretching, a variety of leg and groin exercises, shoulder sit-ups, bicycle pumps, back bends, followed by getting on my feet for neck looseners and arm swivels, claps and flaps, finishing with twenty repetitions of arm lifts with eight-pound weights. A bracing shower and then my inner bugler sounds reveille and the day officially begins with a big glass of fresh orange juice, just as every evening begins with a big gin and tonic. When youngsters in their seventies and eighties, nervously lurching toward the horizon of ninety, ask me, "What's the secret?" That's what I tell them: "O.J. in the morning, gin and tonic at night."

But where and how would I live as a newly minted bachelor? I went through a bleak period of living full-time in New York, trying to establish some kind of social life but I eventually decided I'd be better off jettisoning New York and, in the mode of Henry Thoreau, isolating myself in my big Connecticut house, which is surrounded by several verdant acres. I didn't have Walden Pond but I did have a small reflecting pool that I filled with exotic gold fish and koi. I planted things and cooked things and tried to write things but either you're a Thoreauvian or you're not and, alas, I was far from it. Sitting beside my 12 × 25 reflecting pool with its spitting bird fountain, watching the fish wiggle and glide did not inspire poetic rhapsodies but only made me wish I was gamboling with them.

But I did try valiantly to immerse myself with marigolds, mini-nuggets, mulch, and Miracle-Gro. I ordered twenty-five pedigreed bantam chicks, which came in the ordinary post from Murray McMurray's Hatchery in Iowa, and installed them in a henhouse I had made with an outdoor run. Once they left chickhood, however, and became grownups I lost interest.

I even bought a rather elaborate acrylic paint set from the local art store but my attempts to capture even a whiff of the flora I was trying to paint was pathetic.

One evening, watching a polar bear documentary while eating a Stouffer's unfrozen dinner on a tray, for no discernible reason I began to cry. Yep, tears ran down my cheeks, my nose began to run as a polar bear slid off an ice floe and began to swim. I do not cry easily. In fact, I *never* cry but here I was, slobbering all over myself when there was absolutely nothing to slobber about. I mean, I care about the polar bear's fate as much as the next guy but to cry over?

The following morning, after my inner bugler had reveilled the day, I thought about my tear burst while I was watering the marigolds, and I relegated my polar bear lachrymosity to the realm of bad dreams. Even Henry Thoreau must have had a bad dream once in a while. After all, I was going through a difficult transition, wasn't I? This was not like a fling at retirement, voluntary, nonbinding, this was a whack across my shins, rope around my ankles, quicksand.

Two days later, the tear ducts spilled over as before, again without warning. I had gone to Sue's Tailoring—Sue was a South Korean lady who wields a magic needle—to give me an extra inch in the waist of my trousers and ease the button on my jacket (another depressing development), when, as I stood before the full-length mirror watching her fiddle with my jacket, tears welled up and spilled over.

"Oh, sorry, sorry," Sue said. "I stick you?"

"No . . . no . . ."

"Sorry. So sorry . . ."

"No, Sue," I stuttered, "I stuck myself."

"You have pin?"

"Figure of speech."

"I have Band-Aid . . ."

The previous tearfall was private, but now there was this embarrassing witness. Why in God's name was I crying in that mirror? Sure, letting out one's pants is depressing, but to cry over? Look, Hotch, I said to myself in that full-length mirror, you were a bust as a New Yorker and now you're a bust in Connecticut, so where's the next bust going to be? Coast to coast you can chalk up one bust after another, crying from Mamaroneck to Spokane. And then what?

Even I who likes to pretend he doesn't have a problem when he has a problem had to face the fact that now he had a problem.

I don't exactly recall how I happened upon the name of Dr. Carl B. Brust, practice limited to psychiatric consultation with the elderly. He may have been recommended by someone at the writers' table at Elaine's, or maybe it was one of my kids, tired of looking at my hang-dog face.

I imagined that Dr. Brust would be an elderly gentleman who would exude empathy for my tearletting. His office was in Manhattan between Madison and Fifth in the Sixties. I had trouble finding it because it was five steps below street level, in the basement of a renovated brownstone. The door, located beneath the street stairs, listed five doctors who occupied individual warrens that had been scalloped out of the basement. Probably psychiatrist row.

The Dr. Brust door read, ENTER WITHOUT KNOCKING. I waited in a cramped anteroom whose only ornament was a framed picture of the Colosseum, symbolic for the elderlies, I would guess, broken but still standing.

Dr. Brust was not a mature gentleman, exuding empathy. He was very tall, very fit, immaculately groomed, exuding nothing. He sported a three-pointed white jacket handkerchief, a black and white bow tie and brown and white wingtip shoes. The consultation room was not much bigger than the waiting cubicle. We sat facing each other; when he crossed his long legs his wingtips invaded my space.

I told him my story and he listened impassively, without question or comment, his wingtips switching places once or twice. He did not have a pen and pad in his lap, just kept his gaze steady on my face. Unnerving. Only when I wound up with an account of my tearful finale did he comment.

"Most of my patients shed those unexplainable tears," he said.

I was glad to hear I had company.

"You cry because you are disconnected with your inner self, which has abandoned you. It is the guardian of your psyche, your moods, your tears and so much else. We must find it and reconnect you. Do you meditate?"

"You mean on purpose? Like the Hindus? No, not really."

"What about yoga?"

"I play tennis instead."

"Yoga has restorative positions that would be good for you."

He picked up a folder from a table beside his chair. "Here

are some drawings of yoga positions that are conducive to meditation. Especially the lotus position. Wander your thoughts. Gently. Everything gently. I'll see you Tuesdays and Thursdays, three o'clock."

That afternoon, I put a cushion on the floor of my bedroom and followed the directions on my lotus card. Legs straight out, bend your right knee and put it over your left thigh, then bend your left knee and put it above your right thigh. Put your hands on top of your knees. Folding my knees made a crackling sound and my stretched thighs hurt. I closed my eyes, as instructed, took deep breaths and hoped that my wandering mind would start me on my way to my inner self. No such luck. All it led me to was a replay of the previous night's Yankee game when A-Rod came to bat with the bases loaded, one out, one run behind, and weakly grounded into a double play.

I tried to push A-Rod and the dismal game out of my meditation but after fifteen minutes I gave up, opened my eyes, and tried to stand up but my legs were locked together. I tried to extricate my right foot but it stayed firmly nestled under my left thigh as if someone had glued it in that position. By rolling over and attacking my incarcerated legs from the underside, I finally unwound myself but my legs were numb and when I eventually regained my feet I discovered I had a charley horse.

⁓

I spent three weeks with Dr. Wingtips, Tuesdays and Thursdays, searching for my inner self but I really didn't know for what I was looking. I tried several of those yoga positions that Wingtips thought might induce the kind of meditation that would lead me inwardly, but nothing worked. The Thursday he suggested I read Shirley MacLaine's reincarnation book, *Out on a Limb,* and try meditating about the possibility of my own reincarnation as a way to lead me to my inner being—that was the farewell session in the subterranean cubicle on Sixty-third Street.

For several weeks I was nicely distracted by a musical comedy I wrote with my longtime friend, Cy Coleman, that was in rehearsal at the Coconut Grove Playhouse in Florida, but after the musical opened and I returned to New York I settled back into living on the dark side of the moon.

Until . . .

I was in Bloomingdale's buying Jockey underwear when, at an adjoining counter, I recognized an old friend I had not seen for many years. We embraced, happily thumping each other's back. Dr. Norman Kelman was his name, as endearing a man as I had ever known.

We went across the street to have a coffee. Norm was a distinguished analyst whose roots were embedded with the early Freudians. He had written many important academic works. Now in his upper eighties, I had heard he was still practicing because a tempestuous divorce had left him cruelly strapped.

Norm had a round, receptive face that radiated good fellowship, and his easy laughter was infectious. We reminisced, inquired about each other's progeny, and in telling about ourselves we realized we were in similar limbo, although because of his age (I was a young seventy-seven at the time), I considered his limbo more serious than mine. I began to tell him about my current state when the thought struck me: "Norm, it's probably not possible . . . I mean, I don't know if you might consider . . . What I'm trying to say is, would it be feasible, despite our personal relationship, that you could see me professionally?"

He laughed his marvelous deep-throated laugh. "You mean, could I be objective, dispassionate? Don't know. Never came up before"

"I would like to give it a try."

"All right, let's do." He took a small, leather appointment book from his pocket. "How about next Monday, eleven thirty?" He scribbled down his address.

"I'll be there."

"It may be only that one session."

It turned out to be three months of sessions, Norm's alchemy pulling me up and away from the depressing slope I was on, made slippery by my real and figurative tears.

Without seeming to lead me, he led me through the dark maze of my doubts, helping me to arrive at an open clearing.

Norm's consultation room was large and airy. He wore the same vintage corduroy jacket every day with a paisley vest and one of three alternating knit neckties. He wore brown leather shoes, not wingtips. In Freudian fashion, he would light up a cigar at the start of our sessions and puff on it while I had my say. On good days he would be sharp and insightful, but on days when his patient load was heavy, starting at six A.M., he would sometimes nod off, his chin descending on his chest with his burning cigar dangling from his lips, ash tumbling down his chest. I thought if I stopped talking he might awake, but it had no effect. Precisely at the forty-five minute mark, Norm would straighten up, brush the ashes off his vest and resume puffing as if he had not had his little catnap. He would then devote our last minutes to observations and questions in preparation for the next session when he would make up for lost time.

Looking back on it, I'd say what I cherish the most from those sessions with Norm was what I finally understood about loving, stemming from reliving the arid years of my loveless marriage. "You see, Hotch," Norm had said, "the love you give is the love you get."

It had been a while since our last session, when I decided to tell Norman about the good turns my life had taken and how much he had contributed. I phoned him, intending to invite him for lunch or a drink, but the operator came on and said the number I was calling was out of service. I knew what that meant.

After I hung up, I sat beside the phone for a long time and grieved for him. He was a splendid man who had touched something in me that had elevated my life; that something was the importance of loving, full out and unconditional.

Every time I smell the aroma of a good cigar, I think of Norman.

People ask me what I'd most appreciate
for my eighty-seventh birthday.
I tell them, a paternity suit.

—GEORGE BURNS

Beware of Animal Crackers
in Your Soup

~

Sailing uncharted seas is always a risky business but especially so when the skippers are in their seventies and eighties and have no idea where they are headed. I am speaking of those who have been cast adrift by divorce or demise of a mate. After observing a period of emotional recuperation, often accompanied by declarations of everlasting celibacy, there ensues attempts by relatives and close friends to perform what they perceive as their duty to provide someone to fill the void created by your departed.

This usually involves assurances that you only have to "say hello, that's all" to someone who is also "in your boat—you have a lot in common." Ninety-nine times out of a hundred this meeting is a bust. I am speaking from painful experience. Although after a nettlesome transition, I was relatively pleased with my divorce freedom, I finally succumbed to the nagging blandishments of an insistent, well-meaning friend and agreed to come to a dinner to meet a woman who was "just my type." I had no idea who constituted "my type," but on the evening of the dinner I was asked to pick up my type.

When she came to the door of her Park Avenue apartment, with heavily lacquered hair, tight designer dress, heavy jewelry on all available surfaces, I was glad I had arranged for the taxi to wait, insuring, I hoped, a prompt departure. But she trumped me with already arranged hors d'oeuvres and wine. She instructed the doorman to dismiss the cab, displaying a take-charge mentality.

The living room, where I was seated, was ornately furnished with objects, she informed me, she and her late husband had procured during their extensive travels, each item with a pedigree she copiously dwelt upon.

"You know," she said, "we were having drinks same as we are now, he was seated in your chair, and I was speaking to him at length but when I asked him a question and he didn't answer, I realized he had died but he was sitting up straight, as you are, with his eyes as wide open as yours are."

"We shouldn't be late," I said, standing up, quickly extricating myself from her husband's death chair.

"No, wait," she said, thrusting a cracker at me, "you *must* try my chicken liver, bacon mousse. It was one of my husband's favorites."

For most of the evening—in the taxi and all through dinner—she told me how much I reminded her of her dearly departed. That we both played tennis at our ages, both born in June, both writers (he wrote brochures for MetLife), both from Missouri, and so on, which I partially escaped by trying to converse with the woman on the other side of me.

I was subjected to one final barrage in the taxi taking her back to her apartment. I turned her over to the doorman, thanked her for the evening, and started to shake her hand, but she took my hand and pulled me over to her and kissed me smack on the lips.

"You have my number," she said.

I said, yes, I did, and ducked my head back into the taxi as the doorman led her to the entrance.

I leaned back in the cab, feeling like I had just run a brisk mile, but I have to admit that the chicken liver mouse was pretty damn good.

It was a long time before I got talked into another such invitation. When you are an available single man of mature years you are in demand to even out a dinner table. On this occasion, I was introduced to my intended—a bosomy woman named Belvedere, blonde hair streaked with white or vice versa I can't remember which—at the dinner party so preliminary contact was avoided.

I drove her home, however, and against my better judgment, I accepted her invitation to have a nightcap. Upon entering her small apartment, she activated her record player that loudly produced Shirley Temple singing "Animal Crackers in My Soup."

"I simply adore this recording, can't get enough of it," Belvedere announced while pouring wine. I found this a puzzling infatuation since the song harked back to the forties and you would think that by now it would have faded from Belvedere's hit parade. At first I didn't feel one way or another about little Shirley and her crackers, but in no time I began to detest her because the player had been rigged to keep the song going and going endlessly: "Animal crackers in my soup / Monkeys and rabbits loop the loop / Gosh, oh gee! but I have fun / Swallowing animals one by one" on and on and on.

I got to my feet, prepared to bid Belvedere a hasty goodbye, but she had disappeared and I was stuck with my empty glass and Shirley's cloying little voice going round and round.

When Belvedere finally reappeared she had let down her hair and changed into a long silk robe with feathers at the neck and wrists. She was carrying a bottle of champagne that she handed to me to open while she lowered the lights. I put down the bottle, intending to make a quick getaway, but she suddenly grabbed me and pulled me to her.

"Let's dance," she said.

"To Shirley?" I croaked.

She thrust her cheek against mine, her body glued to me. She started to sing a duet with Shirley in my ear, her off-key alto besting Shirley's little girl flutter. Her neck feathers were tickling my nose. I tried to extricate myself but she was locked onto me. She and Shirley were singing: "In every bowl of soup I see / Lions and tigers watching me / I make 'em jump right through a hoop / Those animal crackers in my soup . . ."

I erupted with a violent sneeze, a few of the feathers flying into space.

"Animal crackers in my soup / Monkeys and tigers loop the loop . . ."

A second sneeze sent a second batch of feathers flying and momentarily Belvedere slackened her hold.

"Osprey," she said, plucking one of the feathers off my shoulder.

Saved by allergies, I squirmed away from her, tears popping from my eyes.

"I have to be home by twelve," I blurted, one of the most idiotic things I ever said, but if I had heard one more loop the loop I likely would have bludgeoned Shirley . . . and maybe Belvedere.

I never filled out another table.

The freedom of being single and unencumbered is not as appealing to the aging bachelor and bachelorette as it was when they were much younger. The bars and clubs and other such gatherings of their youth no longer entice them, so companions have to be found by other means. The Internet is a favorite but photos can be doctored and descriptions enhanced. Some universities have alumni listings, Harvard,

Yale, and Brown among them, but it is still advisable to approach a listing as you would a used car.

I have a good friend, Drew, who was weary of his divorced freelancing, but wary of the ladies who appeared on his ivy school listing. After an initial phone call, if promising, Drew wanted to have a face to face but not involve himself for the entire evening with a woman who fell short of his expectation. For insurance, Drew established a set of hand signals with the waiters whom he knew at Elaine's, a trendy restaurant that then existed on the Upper East Side in New York.

Drew would invite the Internet candidate to meet him at the restaurant. After she was seated and drinks were being ordered, Drew sent a signal to the waiter:

1. The lady is a no-no [FIST] bring a check with the drinks.

   or

2. I'm not sure [FLAT HAND DOWN] bring a second round.

   or

3. We are staying for dinner [HANDS CLASPED] take your time.

None of the restaurant's regulars ever impinged on Drew's courtship table that had fist ladies more often than not. This went on for almost a year, but then one evening when I was dining at Elaine's I was surprised to see that he was having dinner with a woman I had seen at his table before. On my way out, he called me over to introduce me to her. Not too long after that, I received an invitation to his wedding that took place, naturally, at Elaine's.

Devoted friends, Internet connections, church socials, fellow volunteers, are all fertile sources for seniors looking for someone with a minimum of hang-ups and a propensity to hang out, but, for me, happenstance, lady luck, fate, call it what you will, is the best intermediary. Someone I know met his ladylove on the ferry to Staten Island, helping her find a fallen earring. Other fortuitous meetings I know about: in a theater in a mix-up over seating; the heel of a shoe caught in a sidewalk grate; an Arthur Murray tango class; an AA meeting; the voting line; a veterinary's waiting room.

As for myself, I was in limbo after my first wife had died from cancer. I had no luck with the solicitude of friends but great luck going against the odds. I have a pied-à-terre in Manhattan in a large apartment building, with five hundred and twenty condominiums and four elevators. On this particular occasion back in 1993, I was waiting for an elevator, having just retrieved a package from the concierge's desk; an elevator door opened, and as those aboard were dispersing, a recognizable voice said, "Hotch?" The voice belonged to a woman I had not seen for almost thirty years. We had met in

New York, she an aspiring young actress, me a late-blooming playwright. She had the graceful mien of a ballet dancer, and a quiet dynamic that I had discerned in accomplished actresses. On her own, she was able to obtain an audition for the prestigious, exclusive Actors Studio, and her remarkable talent earned her immediate membership.

Over the following year, we had a fine time together and were very much in love, the scruffy St. Louis renegade from the questionable side of the tracks and the Atlanta beauty whose ancestors' names grace the boulevards and parks of Atlanta. But, as good as it was, we had to part when a script of mine went into rehearsal in Hollywood, and she got cast in the touring company of a Broadway play. There was nothing sweet about the sorrow of our parting.

We had not seen each other for those thirty years, but we had written occasionally—she to tell me of her marriage to a prominent stage director with whom she had a son, me to tell her of my marriage in 1970 and the birth of my son, a year or two after hers. We had never met again until that afternoon when that elevator brought us back together. Virginia is her name, and she had recently arrived from Hollywood to live in New York and was in my building looking at an apartment. What are the odds against that confluence?

Married now, we've been together for twenty splendid years, Virginia and I, the point being, no matter your age, there is someone for you, just keep believing. *Pazienza,* the

Italians say, *pazienza*. The days dwindle down to a precious few, but you can certainly make the most of them. Contrary to the cynics who maintain that life, unlike the theater, has no second acts, after an entr'acte of thirty years, my life does have a lovely second act, and the love I now give is overmatched by the love I get.

We don't stop playing because we grow old;
we grow old because we stop playing.
—George Bernard Shaw

Over Your Shoulder and
onto the Green

———

There comes a point in your chronological progression when, assailed by strictures emphasizing the importance of exercise, it becomes increasingly more difficult to keep your body doing what it has always done. Repairs and replacement of moving parts have something to do with it, as does a faltering indecision tugged between participating in physical activity and watching others strut their stuff on television. Nature's cruel anomaly is that exercise slows down the aging process but the aging process slows down exercise.

Although football, soccer, baseball, volleyball, and basketball keep us occupied in our early years, they fade with the approach of middle age, and by the time we enter what is sappily called our "senior years," even modest sports become a memory. Of course, there are rare exceptions, like the aged marathoners who wheezily push their varicose veins over the finish line just before dark. And there is a ninety-two-year-old Canadian, Olga Kotelko, who holds seventeen world track records in her 90–95 age group, her specialties being javelin and shot put, but, as you can imagine, her competition is rather sparse.

The recreational sports that seem to have survived the aging cut-off are golf and tennis but even they show telltale signs of significant shrinkage from age seventy on up. There was a tennis player I once knew, Steve Ogilvy, who trumpeted his reaching the finals of tournaments for those like himself in their nineties. But when questioned he admitted that there were only two participants in the tournament, which meant that on paying his entry fee, he was automatically in the finals.

There comes a time in the life of every sometime golfer when he tees up, looks down the fairway, and suffers the illusion that it has been considerably extended since the last time he played there. In reality his drives have become considerably shorter, and land in the rough more often. He is further aggravated by a perception that the sand traps have become wider and deeper, and the water hazards have been moved closer to the greens. All of which tend to dampen his enthusiasm for rising early on Sunday for a seven o'clock tee time.

It is in the spirit of resuscitating that enthusiasm that I propose certain changes in the rules that will make the game more accommodating to aging golfers. A program is already in place, called Tee It Forward, which proposes to "put the fun back into golf." A million golfers defected from the links last year, super seniors a segment of them, and Tee It Forward wants to lure them back by allowing players to tee off much closer to the hole.

There is another program called Flogton ("not golf" spelled backward), that is endorsed by the Alternative Golf Association. In addition to shortening the tee-off distance, Flogton advocates using tees on the fairways, conceding third putts no matter how far from the hole, using one mulligan on every hole on any one shot, moving the ball six feet in any direction, and if trapped allowing ninety-year-olds to wind up and pitch it as far along the fairway as they can.

To further seduce the wayward, aging linkster, the Polara golf ball that spurns slices and hooks and maintains a straightaway path down the fairway should be allowed, and the rules regarding those unforgiving sand traps should be amended to permit the sand to be smoothed beneath the ball and eighty-year-olds-on up could tee it up.

There's not much concession that can be made about the beastly water hazards other than to permit age-challenged golfers to stand at water's edge with their backs to the greens and pitch the ball over their shoulders.

As for the scorecards, there is absolutely no honor among the older set and the hard-and-fast rule should be that no super senior is to be trusted with his own scorecard. On the other hand, no one in the foursome can be trusted with keeping a competitor's scorecard, so there's a dilemma I'll leave to someone else.

I don't expect these innovations will get a ringing endorsement from the USGA, but according to Descartes and his buddies it takes time for the seed of revolution to grow.

Which brings me to tennis. I have been a devotee of the game since I was twelve years old. I learned to play with busted rackets that had been discarded at the public tennis courts in St. Louis' Forest Park. I became adept at resuscitating demised rackets with strings of cat gut and glue. We had scarcely enough money for food in that baleful epoch of the Great Depression, sometimes not enough for that, so my only tennis lessons were self-administered by hitting a ball for hours against a concrete slab. Tennis remained a constant companion all through my life. Wherever I lived, tennis lived there with me: the Foro Italico in Rome, the Queen's Club in London, Roland Garros in Paris, Club de Deauville in Normandy, clubs in Easthampton and Beverly Hills. I was an average club player but tennis was a passport in these places. My game stayed at a solid level that I took for granted until that doomsday when I realized that what I had always taken for granted was no longer granted. I was not quite reaching balls I had invariably reached; I could no longer get to the net behind my serve; balls at the net were getting quickly past me; returns on my serve were coming a bit harder than the balls I served. This was not precipitous, mind you, but it was the handwriting on the tennis wall.

It was not comforting to realize that what was happening to my game was happening to millions of tennis players all over the world. My misery did not profit from company, The choice was simple: donate my rackets, sweat bands, and Nike tennis shoes to Goodwill or soldier on, implementing my waning skills with cunning, guile, and anticipation. If you were having trouble getting to the ball, then anticipate where it's going and move before it gets there. As my aging deficiencies increased, I surrendered singles to doubles, and that brought on a new challenge: getting a group of players together who played at relatively the same level.

At first that was not difficult, but as they got older, members of that group began to drop like autumn leaves. Herb refused to undergo two new knees, Arnold fatally succumbed to cigarettes, Chet moved away, Hilton passed on for reasons unknown, Frank decided not to replace his busted guaranteed lifetime hip replacement, George renounced tennis and dedicated himself to golf, Gordon deferred to mixed doubles with his wife at his country club, Pete developed a heart murmur.

All over the tennis spectrum, gentrifying players are forsaking the game because they have changed but the game has not. So, like golf, I have a few suggestions that may tempt potential nonagenarian defectors to stay put.

- Eliminate the foot fault and allow the server to start from one stride inside the baseline.
- Allow the server three serves instead of two.

- Lower the net two inches.
- Move all outer lines two feet inward thereby reducing the amount of court requiring coverage.

Bowling is an option but there have been instances when the mature (I prefer that to "senior") bowler fails to disengage his hand from the bowling ball and gets carried along toward the pins, attached to the bowling ball. Also there are times when the bowler can't stop his wobbling momentum and winds up in the alley after releasing the ball. In addition to those hazards there is what the weight of a bowling ball does to a cranky back and a wishy-washy wrist.

Incidentally, I long ago decided never to watch an old-timers baseball game. Whether at the stadium or on television, the impact of seeing the men who were once your heroes, in states of utter decrepitude, limping up to the foul line, their bellies preceding them, tipping their caps to reveal bald pates, close-ups of wrinkled faces that defy your search to find any semblance of recognition, will make you doubt whether you should even bother with physical exercise. The star center fielder who covered the outfield like a gazelle, now leaning heavily on a cane. The third baseman with the arm of a howitzer, now barely able to lift his cap. The Hall of Fame pitcher who goes out to the mound to throw out the first ball, bouncing it twenty feet in front of home plate. And to top it off, these old-timers play for two innings, during which no one can hit, field, or run. No, better not to curdle your recollections of their halcyon days.

There are a number of less organized physical venues that can be pursued. For the physically timid, treadmills can be slowed down to accommodate a very slow walk, and the wheel of a stationary bike can be made to rotate with a very slight push. A friend of mine, smitten with the idea of maintaining his physique despite the inroads of age, installed a succession of conditioning devices in a room in his apartment: a StairMaster, treadmill, bike, rowing machine, wall pulleys, belly vibrator, leg weights, arm weights, medicine ball, but he never used any of them, settling for sitting in a vibrating lounge chair that he obtained from Brookstone. He's now in a nursing home where they do exercises standing in the shallow end of the swimming pool.

As for me, I am still on the court three times a week, playing with youngsters in their seventies and eighties, trying to keep the ball in play. Come to think of it, that is my modus vivendi: Keep the ball in play.

A man is not old until regrets take
the place of dreams.
—JOHN BARRYMORE

If You Can't Pet 'Em,
Don't Get 'Em

———

Television is an inanimate box that displays animate objects of infinite variety, but what it cannot provide for a person of years, who has been reduced to living alone, is companionship; it fills many empty hours, but it does not fill an empty room like a living object. Sometimes one who is cast adrift by a late evolving divorce or the passing of a mate has the good luck of having a family dog or cat for company, but for many of those cast adrift, like myself, such was not the case; my divorce, although welcome, left me rattling alone in my big Connecticut house, feeling isolated.

My three children had long ago left home and established independent lives, and although I had enjoyed a succession of pets for most of my life, there hadn't been one for several years. When the children were young, there were rabbits and lambs and chickens and peacocks, Lanny, a rambunctious red horse, and two Sicilian burrows, Jackie and Jenny, that my daughters, blue-ribbon riders, amazed equestrians at the nearby Fairfield County Hunt Club, by saddling them up and teaching them how to jump over three-foot fences.

But mostly there were wonderful dogs, notably Pango, a handsome Bedlington terrier of extraordinary intelligence, and Pookie, a Lhasa apso, who could fetch a variety of objects from a pile when identified ("get Mickey Mouse" or "bring the yellow bone").

If there had been a Pango that would have nicely sufficed, but I told my kids, who were concerned about me, that I felt no need for a four-legged companion. They overruled me, however, and decided I must have a resident buddy. I insisted that things were just fine as they were, but, to be honest, I was feeling a bit lonely and unhinged. I made it clear, however, that I was not up to going through the rigors of breaking in a puppy. Also, the prospect of having to put a sweater and leash on a dog and walk him through rain, ice storms, snow, heat, all the while trying to keep my balance and fend off inhospitable canine visitors, did not appeal to me. And besides, I pointed out, I go to New York two or three days every week and who would take care of him? I made it adamantly clear that I was enjoying my aloneness and no nurturing quadruped was welcome, but they didn't believe me.

I decided I could preempt their inevitable choice by acquiring a pet that might be tolerable. Cats were out of the question. You're either a cat person or you're not, and I was a confirmed non-catophile. The event that solidified my feline antipathy had occurred years earlier. I was living in New York, involved with a young soprano of the Paris Opera, whom I had met when, toward the end of World War II, I had received my honorable discharge in Paris as a major in the air force. The young soprano, whose name was Elena, had come to New York for several performances at the Met. She had brought with her a black Persian cat with violet eyes, named Annie, that she adored. When she had to temporarily return to Paris to sing *Tosca* at the Paris Opera, she entrusted Annie to my care with strict instructions as to her needs and sensitivities. Elena was gone for three weeks and they were three weeks in the hotter recesses of hell. From tip to tail Annie was grand opera. She flashed demonic eyes at me, cat woman that she was, hissed and refused to use her kitty box. When she started to scratch rips in the silk sofa, I tried to stop her and she scratched me instead. No matter which of her many prepared diets I fed her, she overturned the bowl onto the carpet and ate the offering from there, grinding her food into the carpet in the process. In the dead of night, she sometimes suddenly awoke, howling and hissing and running in rambunctious circles around the room. The one time she was lying on the sofa, placid and comfortable, and I went over to stroke her beautiful head, she dug her teeth into my forefinger. I slapped her and she howled for twenty minutes while I was treating my wounds with Neosporin and a Band-Aid.

When Elena came back, Annie sailed into her arms, mewing and cuddly. "She's lost weight," Elena said, accusingly. "Well, no matter, I have rehearsals for *Carmen* and interviews and I have no time for a cat. Here, Helen," she said to the cleaning woman, "here's this nice kitty for you."

To forestall the universal wrath of the cat people, let me reiterate my acknowledgment that there are multitudes of cat people happy with their lot, although I have witnessed many cat people summon their lovelies with enticing words and bonbons only to be snubbed.

But I digress. I decided to find a pet I'd be happy with, thereby taking the offensive away from my daughters who were obviously hell-bent on interfering with my life. I visited a pet store to size up possibilities, but while I was mulling over tropical fish, finches, hamsters, a boa constrictor, white rats, a monkey, turtles, a de-skunked skunk, and so forth, my daughters beat me to it.

They called a day after our pet powwow to announce they had solved my predicament.

"I have no predicament."

"We are sending you a young African Gray Parrot who will be arriving this Friday at Kennedy Airport."

"He's flying in?"

The parrot was coming from a breeder in Spokane, Washington, and would be transported to me in Connecticut. I asked why a parrot was coming all the way from Spokane when there were certainly plenty of local parrots.

"The breeder is a friend of ours—we wouldn't think of getting you a parrot from a stranger."

The African Gray is the prince and princess of parrots. Macaws are more colorful, Cockatoos more beautiful, but the African Gray is a talker with a high IQ and a familial disposition. We discussed a name for him and they suggested "Ernest" in honor of Hemingway, my good friend for many years. They sent me an attractive, commodious cage that had a baffle around the bottom that was designed to dissuade the resident from leaving his home turf. I was assured that Ernie required very little attention: Change the food and water once a day and clean the cage once a week. Parrot food was on order to arrive regularly by mail.

Ernie bore his journey nobly and established himself quickly in his new home. Although mostly a luminous gray, he has a bright red tail and wide, white circles around both eyes. He has since acquired an extensive vocabulary, around 250 words and phrases, all of which he has learned only from me and he speaks with my voice. He sings, whistles tunes, and when the phone rings, says hello and gives my telephone number.

I have had Ernie for many years and he has taken over the house as well as my wife, Virginia, and me. In the morning when I come into his room, from under his cover he calls out, "Bonjour, comment-allez-vous, je suis bien." When I open the cage door he comes out and goes to one of his many perches. In addition to his parrot food, he eats everything I eat and if there is something on my plate that he covets, he lets me know it. He particularly likes potatoes, tuna fish, cheerios, cheese, spaghetti, iced tea, peanuts, ice cream, jelly beans, French toast, pancakes, grapes, smoked salmon, hamburgers, potato chips, asparagus, croissants, and chicken; there are only two things he must not eat: chocolate and avocado, both deadly.

At night I open his door and tell him: "I'll see you tomorrow," and he goes into the cage by himself. I cover him and from under the covers he says, in my voice, "I'll see you in the morning."

During the course of the day he often amazes me with new vocabulary that is sometimes unexpected. Two proper ladies came to visit one day, and he said, "Hello, I love you," when they came into the room where he dwells. But when they drew near to him, saying, "Oh what a darling bird!" he said, in my voice, "Kiss my ass."

His linguistic inventions and his comments are constantly diverting. Like a child, when not pleased he sometimes throws his food. I scold him. He sulks. But he delights in being stroked and it is easy to get back in his good graces. I have a friend who has an African Gray that lets himself out of his cage every morning around seven o'clock, crosses his room and goes up the stairs to my friend's bedroom, climbs up the bed, and pulls away the covers, waking my friend in time to get to work.

When I'm alone with Ernie, I'm not alone. He does not have to be walked, boarded, or bathed. He washes himself from his water cup and when I go to New York, I leave him an ample supply of food and water. I have a small carrying case so I can take him with me whenever I wish. He likes to travel and meet new people. I don't have to guess what he's thinking—he tells me. In the evening, when I have a drink before dinner, he will call for carrots or peanuts or celery or simply say, "Bring me something." He only says this at drink time. He knows. When I put on my coat and go out the door, he says, "See you later—bye bye," and when I come back he says, "Hi sport, welcome home." He came up with a new expression today when I gave him a piece of watermelon: "Okey-dokey, yum-yum."

Grays commonly reach one hundred, so Ernie will surely outlive me—I have him in my will. I don't know if there are a sufficient number of African Grays to fill the lives of all the lonely seniors, but I hope so. I assure them they won't feel lonely when they are in their favorite chair reading, and they've got a feathered friend sitting on their shoulder singing "Yankee Doodle."

I am long on ideas but short on time.
I expect to live only to be a hundred.

—THOMAS EDISON

You Are Who You Are
Until You Aren't

———

There comes a time in the lives of all parents when they are no longer parents. The exact time of transition varies but it occurs shortly after the child kicks open its cocoon and establishes a nest of its own in a place of its own choosing, a job, income, and INDEPENDENCE. To attenuate the loss of the child, the parent may try to supervise and contribute to the furnishing of the nest and the embryonic bank account, but this is a mistake.

The child, no longer a child, does not want monogrammed towels or a leather Eames chair with a foot hassock to match, no, he/she does not need cash, thank you, nor any of the stuff from the ancestral manse. You quickly learn not to give advice unless asked and that rarely happens. At best you become buddies, pals, occasionally going to lunch, less often dinners; when the child moves far away, you see each other Thanksgiving, Christmas, and on the occasional birthday.

If the subject of money comes up, it must be addressed very cautiously. You believe in the old saw: Neither a lender nor a borrower be. But when it's your own kids, and it's obvious that their cupboard is pretty bare, anxious though you may be to transfer a few bucks to alleviate the shortfall, you cannot presume that your offspring will welcome your contribution. As puzzling as it may seem, they may prefer starvation than reverting to the ghost of their childhood allowances, but then again the recession has induced many of them to move back in with their parents.

Being dutiful grandparents of a certain age may call for forthright honesty when petitioned for caretaking duties. Little tots, running noisily around the house, spilling their drinks, breaking a vase or two, starting the day very early, calls for a certain stamina grandma/pa may no longer possess. So even though your offspring may think you are slackening your grandparenting duty, you cannot do more than you can do. And the same goes if the grandkids are teenagers who may be more of a chore than the little ones.

But the upside of grandparent duty is that the grandchild could get you going with an iPad, a digital camera, Facebook, Twitter, and maybe even get you to tolerate Jay Z and Lady GaGa. The way I see it, there are three stages of parenting: Stage one, toddler to teenager, you establish and enforce the rules and regulations. Stage two: the offspring move out, sign leases, set up bank accounts, buy stocks, have kids. Mothers and daughters shop together, fathers and sons do sports events. Grandkids do sleepovers. You are pals with your children. Birthdays and holidays are planned, festive events.

But then, during your seventies or eighties, along comes stage three when your kids begin to voice and enforce their concerns about your finances, your ability to drive, especially at night, your medications, your doctor visits, your taxes, your balance (shouldn't you get a cane?), your blood pressure, your cholesterol, your clothes, your rugs, sheets, and towels, your diet, your vitamins—you name it. They even subscribe to a service that puts a bracelet on your wrist with an SOS button that, when activated, immediately alerts an operator who caters to your any emergency.

One of your daughters "helps" you throw out a lot of your clothes because, she proclaims, they are "tired." You try to defend every jettison but your efforts are feeble and she prevails. You do not consult him, but one son insists on going over your financials with you, and following his sister's lead, advises you to get rid of stocks and hedge funds that are also "tired."

Red alert! Now is the moment, assuming you are sound of body and mind, you must mobilize your defenses, stand tall, resist inroads, preserve your own way of life! Failure to do so will surely lead to stagnation, assisted living, game shows, apple juice, *Reader's Digest,* group calisthenics.

We superannuated voyagers who have bravely guided ourselves through the treacherous shoals of a long life of living, we are now the upper class, garbed in the proud raiment of survival, free of ambition, relatively content, wise, devoted, reaping emoluments. For us there is still a good hunk of life to live, and by God we're going to live it.

If you want to bungee-jump or canoe the white water or learn to ride a motorbike, go ahead. A ninety-year-old on the beginners' slope, why not? You've always been tempted to experience the thrill of soaring through the sky on the back of a professional skydiver, who's to say it's too risky when you're in your eighties? They outfit you with your very own parachute, don't they?

So just let everyone know that like Lincoln in his D.C. Memorial, Father Duffy in Times Square, those guys on Mount Rushmore, you are getting older but all of you are doing just fine.

RESOLUTIONS WHEN I COME TO BE OLD

Not to marry a young Woman.

Not to keep young Company, unless they really desire it.

Not to be peevish, or morose, or suspicious.

Not to scorn present Ways, or Wits, or Fashions, or Men, or War, etc.

Not to be fond of Children, or let them come near me hardly.

Not to tell the same Story over and over to the same People.

Not to be covetous.

Not to neglect decency, or cleanliness, for fear of falling into nastiness.

Not to be over severe with young People, but give Allowances for their youthful folleyes, and Weaknesses.

Not to be influenced by, or give ear to knavish tattling Servants, or others.

Not to be too free of advice, nor trouble any but those that desire it.

To desire some good Friends to inform me which of these Resolutions I break, or neglect, and wherein; and reform accordingly.

Not to talk much, nor of myself.

Not to boast of my former beauty, or strength, or favour
    with Ladyes, etc.
Not to hearken to Flatteryes, nor conceive I can be
    beloved by a young woman; et eos qui hereditatem
    captant, odisse ac vitare.
Not to be positive or opinionatre.
Not to sett up for observing all these Rules, for fear I
    should observe none.

—*Jonathan Swift*

To be seventy years young is sometimes far more cheerful and hopeful than to be forty years old.
—OLIVER WENDELL HOLMES

You Are Harboring a Snake
in the AT&T Bushes

~

When you were a little tyke, going off to school on your own, one of the constant admonitions from your parents was "never talk to strangers." Now that you're hovering around ninety, that good advice has been shelved, but it shouldn't. Right there in your living room lurches your telephone filled with oily strangers intent on ripping you off: telemarketers poised to sell you products, cruises, services, charity donations, get-rich schemes, vacation condos, bargain mortgages, Nigerian gold mines, television improvements—you name it, they are selling it, and lonely old parties are buying it, sustaining a billion-dollar-a-year rip-off.

As you get older, the world you live in shrinks. You live alone now. Most of your friends have either expired or moved to Florida where they eventually pass on to that great place in the sky where it is less humid. There are times when television goes stale and an aura of bleakness descends. You burst out in tears at unexpected times, not knowing why. You go to see a psychiatrist who specializes in treating the elderly with these bouts of hopeless isolation. There are no antidepressants that help. You have to struggle out of it on your own. Those who do are stronger for having succeeded. Your children call occasionally when they think of it, but for the most part the outside world does not ring you as once it did, *except* the telemarketers.

"Hello, is this Raymond?"

"Yes."

"Oh, hi, Raymond. I'm Cindy with the Improve Your Credit Card Company. How are you today?"

"I'm fine. Is there something wrong with my credit card?"

"Oh, no, Raymond, but we can improve it."

"You call me by my first name—do I know you?"

"No, it's just that we like to be closely identified with our customers. Like I'm Cindy."

"So what's this about my credit card?"

She has you hooked, now comes the spiel that she has rehearsed under excellent tutelage, a spiel she repeats forty or fifty times a day.

TIP: Even if you have caller ID you can't really tell if it's a telemarketer, but there is a way to deal with it right off the bat. If after you say hello, there is not an immediate response, but a pause while the telemarketer connects, hang up. She will not call back since there was no connection and your number is but one of hundreds being called automatically.

Sometimes if I'm especially annoyed by the interruption, I start a conversation before the telemarketer starts hers.

"Cindy, I'd like to tell you what I was doing when you called. I was helping my sick mother get out of bed to take her medicine. Now would you like to be interrupted by someone like you if you were in the midst of helping your sick mother, thinking this phone call was the one you were waiting for from the doctor you have called?"

You'd be surprised at how contrite and apologetic the Cindys become. I sometimes think I should start a national campaign to incite the elders of America to rise up against the evil of the telemarketers. We would arouse senior Americans to attack all these hustlers, huddled in their little plywood warrens, hundreds in each boiler room, trying to pry money and savings from the elderly. It just might shame some of them to quit their loathsome jobs.

If one of these telephonic marauders does manage to grab your ear and induce a conversation, no matter how taken you may be by his oily gab, no matter how convincing he is that his product or service will improve your lonely life, never let him worm the number of your credit card out of you, especially if he assures you he will only keep it on file while you enjoy an absolutely free trial of whatever he's pitching. My friend Homer, age eighty-six, was hypnotized by a telephonic Svengali offering a free ninety-day trial of a television enhancer that resulted in a series of unauthorized charges to his credit card. After exhausting, protracted combat, he succeeded in getting redemption, but now Charlie has given up answering the telephone altogether.

If I do succeed in starting a national uprising, Seniors vs. Telemonsters, I may be contacting you but I assure you, it won't be by telephone.

Retire? How the hell can a writer retire?
DiMaggio put his records in the book, so did
Ted Williams, and then on a particular good day,
with good days getting rarer, they hung up their shoes.
So did Marciano. That's the way a champ should go out . . .
A champion cannot retire like anyone else.

—ERNEST HEMINGWAY

Out of the Rat Race
and into the Trap

———

When I turned eighty-five, as a present to myself, I decided that after sixty years of writing this and that and peddling salad dressing it was time to retire. I was still physically fit, and, in my estimation, still possessed of all my faculties, but it was a fallow writing period and for all I knew, maybe permanently fallowed. The guys in my tennis group were all retired and so were many of my friends who had moved their retirement away from the harshness and hurly-burly of their working years.

I was not at the point of pulling up stakes and moving elsewhere, but I had not really thought about what I would do as a retiree. A freelance writer all my life (except for the two boring years I practiced law), I had traveled extensively and lived abroad in desirable places, thus travel was not a compelling consideration. I had always been a steady reader so I did not have a backlog of volumes to catch up on. A retired friend who had been a writer said that he had found an absorbing preoccupation with woodworking, making birdhouses, bookends, CD holders, and the like, but in view of the fact that manual training was the only course I flunked in high school—band saws, jigsaws, hacksaws, were not my forte.

I canvassed the retirees I knew to find out if what interested them might interest me. Leo, eighty-four, had joined an all-male senior choral group, The Wise Men, that regularly rehearsed their musical arrangements; they had a full performance schedule at senior centers, nursing homes, prisons, and civic events. I attended one of their performances; they were pretty thin in the tenor section but they had nicely syncopated gestures, matching jackets, and a uniform heartiness. I was a bit tempted to try out, but one thing about me, I am realistic about my many shortcomings, and singing off-key is one of them.

Charlie, eighty-three, enthusiastically described his twice-weekly trips to the poker tables of the nearby Foxwoods Resort Casino, and Dave, eighty-two, enthused about his bridge afternoons (Tuesday contract, Thursday auction), but in either event I could not fathom hitching my retirement to a deck of playing cards.

David, eighty-seven, was deeply involved in photography— ten types of cameras, special lights and reflectors, fully equipped darkroom, exhibition prints—which definitely interested me until he began to describe how he had to reconcile the shutter speed and the light factor to the depth of field and other variables, which reminded me of my military encounter with photography. My first assignment in the air force after graduating Officer Candidate School was as the Adjutant of the 13th Wing of the Antisubmarine Command, an outfit dedicated to searching for Nazi U-boats and blasting them. I had barely wet my wings when the wing's commanding officer informed me that I was to be detached to make a propaganda film extolling the AntiSub Command, which at that time was jousting with the U.S. Navy over who was the designated U-boat hunter. I saluted and said, respectfully, that I knew absolutely nothing about photography, especially shooting movies from a diving B-25. The colonel gave me a look: "Lieutenant," he said, "we all came into the war knowing nothing about nothing."

It had been a harrowing three months trying to capture footage from the nose of a rambunctious medium bomber and another two months putting it together. "Atlantic Mission" turned out good enough to earn me a promotion to first lieutenant but a month after its release the navy was granted exclusivity over the submarine-hunting skies and the Air Force Antisubmarine Command was dissolved, its personnel (including me) scattered to deployment outposts. The ordeal of "Atlantic Mission" was the beginning and end of my interest in photography.

Will, ninety, was a friend who made extraordinary kites and flew them in combative competitions. I spent time in

Will's workshop and developed a real interest in kiting but despite several attempts I could not construct a kite that could fly, much less compete.

Emerson, also eighty-five, who had been in my basic training group at Sheppard Field, Texas, tried to sell me on joining his amateur theater group. He had seen the air force musical, "Three Dots with a Dash," that I co-wrote and in which I performed, and he urged me to try out for a part in "The Torch Bearers," which his group was just then casting. But after touring with "Three Dots" in army trucks and performing in towns all over Texas, Oklahoma, and Kansas, the proceeds going to the Air Force's Widow's Relief Fund, I vowed that performing was not only not in my blood, but actually had curdled it.

I did try a couple of retirement pursuits on my own. I had been impressed with the canvases that Winston Churchill created in his later years and I liked the notion of imitating him and sitting in my garden with easel and palette, imbuing a canvas with whatever inspiration bubbled to the surface. I went to the Fine Arts store on Main Street and loaded up with art supplies, set up my easel, donned a straw Van Gogh–type hat, and went to work. No matter how I blended my acrylics they never seemed to evolve into the color I intended. But that was the least of my disappointments, which centered around the messes I smeared on my brand-new canvases. I tried geometrics like Frank Stella and floating globs of color à la Mark Rothko (they looked more like

Hebrew National salamis) and some freeform stuff in the manner of Helen Frankenthaler but the canvases looked like they had suffered a seizure. I spent endless hours capturing our house on my last canvas. The house is a handsome three-story Normandy-type with a steeply gabled roof, but the end result on the canvas was a weird-looking structure I myself would never inhabit.

Phil, eighty-nine, was an avid stamp collector and he expounded on its virtues, but the only collecting that interested me emotionally was cigar bands. During the Great Depression, when I was twelve, I assiduously combed the gutters and cigar counters of St. Louis searching for cigar bands and the arty designs on the cigar boxes. Cigars were very popular then, and the makers, especially in Havana, tried to outdo one another with their extravagant art. They hired high-priced artists and the colors were vibrant, dominated by gold woven throughout the designs. One of my favorites was the Uwanta Cigar art, featuring an Indian brave in full, colorful regalia, arrows in a beaded container on his back, shield and feathered spear in one hand, his other holding the reigns of his beautiful pony. The bands that I exhumed from the gutters featured gorgeous women (La Coquetta, Speckled Sumatra with a naked breast peeking out of her chemise), military men (General Pershing), opera (*Rigoletto*), actors (Rudolph Valentino, Lillian Russell, Ethel Barrymore), presidents (Franklin Delano Roosevelt), history (*Spirit of St. Louis*), celebrities (Mark Twain, Socrates, Daniel

Boone), and cowboys, Indians, little children, dogs, horses, cats, lions, all with cigars. My absolute favorite was the very elaborate Vandevin Y Hermanos that featured a little blonde, winged angel puffing a cigar while steering a little swan-shaped sailboat afloat on an azure sea, the sail featuring a large pink rose. That collection of mine was, for me, a trove of hidden treasure as rewarding as panned gold, a beautiful collection it was, my pride and joy. It had been kept in a trunk in the basement of Sorkin's Meat Market where we lived in two rooms above the store. When Sorkin's water pipes burst, flooding the basement, all the contents of our trunk, including my cigar band beauties, were waterlogged and ruined.

It was a tearful loss that I still feel after all these years. At a time when food was scarce, the rent on our fleabag hotel room in arrears, our clothes frayed, my mother in a tuberculosis sanitarium, my father on the road trying to sell watches no one could afford, the sparkling gems of my cigar band collection, the envy of other kids who were also collecting, was a bright spot in my life, especially during those hot summer weeks when I had to live by myself in that miserable hotel room, not able to leave the room knowing that if I did, the sadistic bellhop would slap a lock on the door. How often that summer I would go through my cigar bands to fortify my morale, a glittering treasure as good as gold and gems.

But in my retirement there was no way to start a collection that could make up for that long-ago loss. There were collections and rare individual cigar bands that could be purchased, but without the twelve-year-old thrill of discovery and the excitement of swapping with other boys, the purchase would have no more meaning than buying a new shirt. Add to that the fact that cigars are no longer in favor and the wonderful art of cigar bands had long disappeared; even the highly prized Upmann has a plain brown band.

However, I know that, like Phil, there are many super seniors who have found collecting a rewarding pursuit, even a passion. Everything from paperweights to music boxes to restaurant menus to pottery to teapots to almost anything you can think of. I have a friend, ninety-three, who has an outstanding collection of autographed tennis balls, beginning with Bill Tilden's, and he travels to tournaments everywhere to augment his collection. His wife, Molly, goes with him to seek out new restaurants, thereby adding to her trove of menus.

The best example I know that proves the folly of self-imposed retirement based on age is the experience of the Bigelows. They lived near me in Connecticut and Mr. Bigelow commuted an hour or so to his job in New York City. There came a time when he decided that his job and the harsh New England winter weather should be traded in for a leisurely life in Florida. Mrs. Bigelow agreed and they sold their house and relocated.

For a good while, the weather and the golf course rewarded them, but only for a while. The repetition of their days rivaled that of their Connecticut existence, and they eventually found that the sterility of Florida made them yearn for the vitality of New England, cold weather or not. So they opted out of Florida and returned to Connecticut, but, without their house, they had to make do with makeshift lodging and they had no agenda. It was Mrs. Bigelow who suggested that since everyone who came to visit liked the tea she blended, perhaps she could sell it in the local stores. For a name, she suggested that since her tea caused constant comment, they should call it that.

"Constant Comment" caught on in the local stores, and the Bigelows eventually bought one used tea bag machine from Lipton's. Today, in neighboring Fairfield, the Bigelow Tea Company is a well-established national brand that occupies an entire block. Years later the Bigelows retired for a second time, but they did not arbitrarily impose their retirement on themselves at a time when they were not ready for it. It was John Milton who said, "Short retirement urges sweet return."

Arbitrary retirement at preconceived ages, sixty-five being the most common, are often coerced by employers on the theory that an employee slides downhill after that. Even the self-employed and employees with options who are still vitally performing their work, subscribe to the

Holy Grail of sixty-five as the propitious time to give it up, losing sight of the fact that they are scrubbing some of their most productive years. How many justices of the Supreme Court thrived in their later years? College professors? Actors? Picasso? Matisse? Some years ago, I attended a party celebrating the one-hundredth birthday of the legendary musical comedy director, George Abbott, who at that age was in the midst of rehearsals for a new musical comedy. And while we are on the subject of longevity, here is an excerpt that ran in the September 30, 2011, edition of *The New York Times*:

VERY LATE IN HIS CAREER, A COMPOSER TRIES A FLUTE

Elliott Carter completed his Concerto for Flute and Ensemble in March 2008, back when he was only 99. The astonishingly prolific Mr. Carter is about 10 weeks shy of 103. Since he turned 100, he has written 14 works.

The article states that Mr. Carter's language had its usual piercing, atonal bite, but that this score was simpler than earlier ones. The critic said this made it easier for Mr. Carter's "scintillating sonorities, myriad instrumental colors and complex rhythmic interplay to emerge."

The ovation he received induced Mr. Carter to rise, a bit shakily, and acknowledge it.

There are many other superannuated achievers paddling alongside Mr. Carter's boat. Eva Zeisel, one hundred and five, a modernist designer who, as a young woman, spent sixteen months in a Soviet prison camp in the 1930s, recently published her memoirs. Irving Fields, ninety-six, plays piano six nights a week at an Italian restaurant in Manhattan while sipping a vodka martini or two that are on the piano. Yoshihiro Uheida, a ninety-two-year-old Japanese American, coaches judo at San Jose State University. When Irving Berlin turned one hundred, he was asked if it was all right with him if a commemorative event were staged in Carnegie Hall. "What's the hurry?" he replied.

Which, after this lengthy detour, brings me back to my ill-advised arbitrary retirement when I was eighty-five. My chronological years might have indicated retirement, but my mind would have none of it. One morning, nine months into my retirement, I found myself thinking of something that stirred my writing juices; try though I did to banish it, it persisted, and before my eighty-sixth birthday I was scribbling in my notebook (I write longhand), just as now, several years later, I am scribbling this tome that you are reading.

Though our outer nature is wasting away,
our inner nature is being renewed every day.

—2 Corinthians 4:16

Either Use It or Lose It

What you don't want in your tender years are imponderables that pop up out of nowhere. As a super senior you feel secure that you have settled life's important decisions, but along erupts a rather nasty new one: whether to renew your magazine subscription for one year or for two, the latter at a bargain price. Your dilemma is, are you secure or insecure about how long you'll be sitting in your favorite chair reading *The New Yorker* or *Reader's Digest*.

You have already faced a number of similar dilemmas. Whoever said a dilemma only had two horns? There are multi-horned dilemmas that would make a veteran matador run for the *barrera*. Dilemma: Your service garage has presented you with a list of necessary repairs for your eight-year-old Chevy to keep it in running shape. Should you put that hefty amount into your aging Chevy or invest a much heftier amount in a new Malibu you ogled in the showroom?

Dilemma: How long will you be able to drive? Your good friend Roger recently had to surrender his driver's license because he was having trouble finding his way back to his house where he had lived for twenty-four years, and the police were tired of helping him find his way home. Lose your license and you only surrender your patched-up Chevy, not a new Malibu with thirty-six months of extended payments. But then again you may be sound of mind and limb and enjoy years of pleasure tooling around in the Malibu.

Dilemma: The lease on your apartment is up for renewal—which is it, a two-year or a five-year lease at a lower increase? Dilemma: Should you continue to pay dues to clubs and organizations you have belonged to for years but which you rarely go to anymore? Dilemmas abound. You get an unexpected check—spend it or stash it in your savings account?

I solve every dilemma with an unwavering point of view—take the long road: the longer subscription, the longer lease, the new car, all the dues, spend the windfall—where longevity is concerned I throw caution to the wind. I intend to be here for a goodly stretch and that's that.

Your resolve, however, faces more and more challenges the older you get. Your memory skips, your energy zaps, your balance gets dicey, but you've got to believe that with a solid jab, nifty footwork, and a good head fake you can persevere. But there's no denying that your memory does play tricks on you. One day you're on top of your game: the crossword puzzle is a breeze, you have everyone's phone number at your fingertips; the next day you can't remember what you had for dinner the night before. You're in the garage and think of something you have to get on the second floor so you go back into the house and trudge up the flight of stairs to the second floor, but when you get to the top landing you can't for the life of you remember what it was that you came up there to get. You bedevil your brain to no avail. You finally give up, go back to the garage, get in the car, drive a few blocks, and then it finally dawns on you—you wanted to take your gray suit to the cleaners.

My friend Melvin decided to do something about these lapses. He went to Toys "R" Us and bought an Etch A Sketch that he remembered from his childhood, that little mechanical toy you write or draw on with a pointed marker, leaving an impression that can be removed by turning the top upside down and shaking, thereby magically restoring a blank surface. Mel drilled two little holes in the top of the Etch A Sketch, attached a string that he looped around his neck thereby having the slate ready to record his missions, erasing it when the mission was accomplished. Now when Mel is in the garage or the backyard and he remembers something he needs upstairs, he jots down a clue, like "Get sunglasses in coat." All his friends in the Thursday night poker game now have Etch A Sketches hanging around their necks next to their reading glasses. Mel is thinking about contacting the Etch people about his invention.

It is doubtful that Mel's brainstorm will get any further than around the necks of a few of his friends, but there is a memory aid that has caught on with a multitude of super seniors—the ubiquitous Post-It, Minnesota Mining's gift to the nation. By the time you reach ninety you rely on the little stickers for everything, from the time you go to the doctor to the TV program you want to see in the evening. There are Post-Its of different colors on the bathroom mirror, the pillows, the refrigerator door, the windshield of the car, the stove, the front door, the back door, the telephone, the dishwasher, the garbage can, the closet door, the microwave— the house looks like a garden of rectangular flowers bearing messages: Get Drano; Aunt Mary called; Clean spot on tie; Water geraniums; Exchange cousin Grant's present; Church social 6:30; Leave check TV repair; Wash Tonto.

I thought I was immune from these memory lapses until I fell victim to a sudden memory jolt that hit me while I was writing a thank-you note for a Christmas plant that I had received from a friend. I wrote, "Many thanks for the BLANK," a name everyone knows, the plant was right before my eyes, but no matter how hard I concentrated, its name would not emerge. All that day I brooded over my memory lapse, suspecting that my heretofore spot-on recall was now sputtering toward some dire end, perhaps a precursor of Alzheimer's. And to further incite my fear, that same day when talking to someone on the phone, I suggested meeting for a coffee at BLANK!, a name as common as grass. Bumbling, I covered with, "Oh, you know, that coffee place on the corner." I didn't retrieve "poinsettia" on my own, but "Starbucks" did pop up a short time after I hung up.

I immediately sought a consultation with a neurologist about these memory lapses, fearing the worst, but then was relieved to know that after sixty years of age, word retrieval failures were common, often covered by the old cliché—"it's on the tip of my tongue."

I also discovered that as you get older, past your working years, your brain still needs continual stress to maintain or enhance itself, not worry stress, but positive, good stress like playing bridge, poker, board games, learning a new language, going to plays and concerts, traveling, doing crosswords, physical activity, anything that challenges the mind but doesn't frustrate it. Watching *Jeopardy!*, for example, makes your brain feel bad, because even when you know or you think you know the answer the contestant has already rung up his cash before you can untangle your tongue and bark your answer, which is often wrong. Not good that your brain is humiliated like that. But your brain is all smiles when it wins at poker.

"Old minds are like old horses," John Quincy Adams said, "you must exercise them if you wish to keep them in working order."

Nothing delights the brain more than variety. If you have a job or profession that is repetitive, performing the same function day after day, the monotony lulls the brain into a stupor that shortens its run. Working on a book, day after day, months leaching into years may seem like a very repetitive process, but I assure you that creating new pages every day provides my brain with all the torque it can handle. My father, who emigrated here from Poland as a young man, loved aphorisms, which he had a tendency to pluralize: put your noses to the grindstones, early birds catch the worms; variety is the spices of life. I thought of him when I learned that variety was a key contributor to longevity. "Variety," Disraeli said, "is the mother of enjoyment." The more pursuits you engage in, even at the same time, the more the brain strengthens its muscle. The spices of life indeed.

Variety has always been my modus operandi. I have written books, plays, essays, musicals, and movies, often overlapping. And on top of that, I started camps for children with cancer and a charity-driven food company with my old pal, Paul Newman. But that doesn't mean there hasn't been time for kicking back and daydreaming. You never have nightmares in a daydream—only white horses that win the Kentucky Derby by six lengths every time they run.

I'm saving the rocker for the day
I feel as old as I really am.

—DWIGHT EISENHOWER

Coming to the Reunion?
Thanks, but No Thanks.

———

The downside to a college education is the Reunion. Every spring, as sure as daffodils, my alma mater's invitation for the June Commencement would pop up, and every year I would send regrets to the Committee for the '40 Reunion that I would not be able to attend the event. The invitation invariably emphasized the joy of "catching up on things with your old classmates" but that was not a carrot that would entice this old horse to trot back to St. Louis, which is the situs of Washington University. It's not that I am not fond of my dear old alma mater (B.A. and J.D.), I am, but it's simply that I quail at the prospect of having to exchange an accounting of my life with all the inquisitive members of my graduating class, none of whom I had seen or corresponded with since graduation. And, to be honest, I wasn't keen on having to congratulate those classmates who had become professors, judges, senators, and captains of industry who, in my view, had careers that really counted (St. Louisans like to say "made something of themselves."). So I was a successful Reunion Dodger until, beginning in April, I was bombarded with urgent requests that I attend the milestone Fiftieth Reunion. This time, in addition to postal and e-mail exhortation, I was repeatedly telephoned by members of the Reunion Committee, only a few of whom I vaguely remembered. I politely tried to fend them off but what nailed me was a very persuasive call from Sally, who, in my senior year, had been crowned the glamorous Homecoming Queen.

Before departing from New York on the eve of the Commencement, I got out my old, frayed yearbook, and on the plane I studied the faces and identifying text of the 1940 graduates, some of whom I almost remembered. By the time I arrived at the hotel where the Reunion Banquet was going to occur that night, I had convinced myself that this might be an enjoyable experience after all.

I picked up my name tag on the table outside the banquet hall, plastered it on the lapel of my jacket, and bravely stepped into the Cardinal Room where cocktails were being served prior to the dinner itself. Instead of the crowd I had anticipated, there was a rather modest group of about two hundred elderly people (surely much older than I) some with canes, a few in wheelchairs.

A woman, who since graduation must have lived on potatoes and ice cream, waddled over and enthusiastically grabbed my hand. "Oh, Frank!" she enthused, "how wonderful to see you!" For a moment I thought I'd go along with being Frank, but I decided to be myself. I pointed to my name tag to correct her, saying inanely, "I guess after seventy everyone looks the same." She apologized and explained that she was having trouble adjusting to her recent cataract operation.

I barely recognized a few faces but I got adept at scanning name tags quickly. Once I knew the name I searched for vestiges of the face I remembered. I did manage to identify Gus who had written some of the music for the musical comedy, *Down in Front* that I had written during my senior year for the annual Quadrangle Club performance. (The previous year's musical had been written by Shepherd Mead who, in later years, wrote *How to Succeed in Business Without Really Trying*.) There was a piano in the room and I asked Gus to play one of the songs from our show, hoping it would liven things up, but he said, sadly, that arthritis had put an end to his piano-playing days.

A hand mike was passed person to person and we took turns at identifying ourselves and giving a thumbnail summary of our lives, most of my classmates touting their children and grandchildren. When the mike was passed to me, trying to rupture the monotony, I identified myself as Eugene O'Neill and said that since graduation it had been a long day's journey into night. Two classmates snickered. The highlight at my table was the discovery by one woman that her doctor was the son of the woman sitting across from her. That unleashed a torrent of medical exchanges: cataracts, bypasses, hypertension, diabetes, hearing aids, etcetera. A retired architect named Ralph described in detail his ongoing bout with episodic amnesia. Don't ask. There was also a lively exchange of anecdotes about knee, hip, and shoulder replacements. There was more metal at that table than a Mafia convention.

A couple of the Reunionists had brought weathered copies of *Papa Hemingway* for me to sign. A woman, identified on her copious bosom as Gracey, told me how much she had enjoyed my *Grapes of Wrath*.

A tall man labeled Arthur, who said he had been with me in Professor Arnold J. Lein's poli-sci lecture class, tapped his water glass, and read a long poem he had composed that incorporated all of our names. He rhymed Hotch with "notch." I was grateful he had avoided "crotch."

A flowered dress named Hilda cornered me to complain about the Newman's Own oil and vinegar dressing. (She was referring to Newman's Own, a salad dressing business that Paul Newman and I started in 1982 that gives all of its profits to charity.)

"Why can't you have one of those doo-dads on your bottle that goes plop plop plop when you pour instead of like now when it gushes out and drowns my salad?" It was moments like this that made me regret I had strayed from the writing life.

"I'll look into it," I said.

"You're bamboozling me," she protested.

"I don't bamboozle," I said with a touch of annoyance. "Why don't you pour it into a tablespoon and jiggle it on like that?" I couldn't believe I was dispensing salad-dressing wisdom.

"All right," she said, turning away, "I'll try that. But you're going to look into a plop plop plopper, right?"

It didn't end there. When we were seated in the Mississippi Room, the woman to my right, Marge by tag, said she was considering writing her autobiography, beginning with her life on campus, then on to the start of World War II when she had enlisted in the WAC, Women's Aviation Corps, she explained. She started to provide me with details about the WAC but I told her that I had been a major in the air force and I knew all about the women who ferried gasoline and supplies in airborne tankers. She gave me a collegial smile and asked if I would help her with her book-to-be. I said I would be glad to read the finished work but that I wouldn't have time to do more than that since I was busy with a book of my own. She shot me an aggrieved look and transferred her attention to the retired judge on her other side.

Roscoe, a large, hearty man with an uneven mustache whom I did not recall, said he had been in my law school class, and still remembered me as Connie Contract in the seniors' Annual Lampoon. It was a law school tradition that every year the senior class would present a show on the stage in January Hall for the benefit of the faculty (who was skewered) and students. The show he referred to was one that I produced in my senior year. One of the numbers I had written and performed was "Connie Contract's Lament." I had transvestied in a dress I had borrowed from my mother, and a sexy blonde wig that came from the costume collection of Thyrsus, the drama club. To my astonishment, I remembered some of the words to the song, which I chanted for Roscoe.

I'm tired of living a life of sin,
I'm tired of whiskey,
I'm tired of gin.
I'm tired of night life, I guess I'm too old,
I'm just a breached contract, who's out in the cold.

I'm just a breached contract who's partially performed,
Over whose clauses many lawyers have swarmed,
From offer to acceptance my form is still intact,
So don't dare try to get me with an overt act.

After that show, Professor Tyrell Williams, a dignified, beloved senior member of the faculty who taught contracts, came up to me backstage. "Mr. Hotchner," he said, in his gravelly voice, "you're going to be a fine lawyer if you wish, but seeing you up on the stage and reading your column in *Student Life* and your stories in the campus magazine, I think you should give that career serious consideration." After graduation I did start to practice law in St. Louis with a prestigious firm but in my second year I was drafted into the air force, and when I was discharged four years later I took Professor Williams' advice and stayed in New York to try to make my way as a writer.

Capping the evening, the Washington U. Glee Club serenaded us with a medley of campus favorites, and the Chancellor dropped in to thank us for all the fine support we had given the university for the past fifty years. The bright spot for me was seeing that Sally, whose hair had turned a lustrous white, had retained her beauty, and that she had just celebrated her golden anniversary with Bruce who had been captain of the tennis team.

The following day, under a perfect sky, in the lustrous quadrangle that was surrounded with parents and guests, the happy graduates of all the University's schools—engineering, law, arts, medical, social sciences—paraded in and took their places. The commencement speaker spoke to them of hope and promise and courage. Sitting across the aisle from them, I felt a certain pride and affection and compassion for these bright young graduates and my eyes teared up. I guess I was seeing myself sitting there fifty years ago, filled with the same feelings of happiness and ambition and uncertainty, hearing similar words of incitement and encouragement from my commencement speaker, now feeling identified with these young graduates about to start their lives, bringing their dreams and talents into their futures, just as I had brought mine. After this experience I decided that I will attend my class reunion every fifty years.

The longer I live,
the more beautiful life becomes.
—FRANK LLOYD WRIGHT

Kidnap Yourself for
Thirty Minutes Every Day

———

My discovering the joy of napping ranks right up there with the day I discovered I could swim, the day I hit my first home run when I played second base for the Kennard Grammar School team, the morning I put my forefingers in my mouth and surprisingly produced a shrill whistle, and the evening before an intimate gathering of family and friends when Virginia said, "I do."

In my pre-superannuated years, I regarded the nap as a sissy failure to go the distance, and besides, I was convinced I wasn't capable of sleeping during the day. Even when I was in the Officer Candidate School of the Air Force and drew overnight guard duty (we patrolled the shores of Miami Beach where a Nazi mini-sub had landed and disgorged several disguised agents with terrorist paraphernalia), I was not able to take advantage of the two-hour morning nap we were allotted.

So it was indeed a revelation when, while sitting at my desk trying to straighten out a crooked sentence, I unwittingly lowered my head onto my arm and took twenty minutes off the clock. I was a youngster of eighty then, and I have embraced that miracle of refreshment ever since, what Shakespeare called "nature's soft nurse." As needed as the intermission of a Wagnerian opera, the nap gathers up the loose threads of the day and entwines them for the evening. Some naps are unintentional, involuntary escapes from a surfeit of boredom. Such a nap, George Bernard Shaw said, "is a brief period of sleep which overtakes superannuated persons when they endeavor to entertain unwelcome visitors or to listen to scientific lectures."

The voluntary nap has been a contributing fixture in the lives of many men of achievement: Mark Twain, Thomas Edison, Edgar Allan Poe, Salvador Dalí, Richard Wagner, John Ruskin, Rembrandt—to name a few. They invented ways to limit the length of their naps, for if a nap is too long it becomes a sleep, thereby blunting the effectiveness of its briefness. Dalí's solution was to set himself in his favorite chair, a large brass key in his hand, and a metal plate under his feet. His nap would end when his hand relaxed and dropped the key onto the plate. Thomas Edison had a similar solution, putting metal plates on the floor, holding a metal ball in each hand, and awakening when his hands relaxed and dropped the balls.

My nap procedure is less primitive but not as original.

When I first embraced napping, I set a little kitchen timer to thirty minutes, but now repetition has conditioned me to awake automatically without being prodded by the timer. The nap can be set for whatever time suits the napper, but more important are the requisites that induce the nap. A comfortable, familiar setting in a favorite easy chair or daybed with one of those vibrating heating pads that can be placed anywhere. A sleep mask is also a good ingredient as is music that doesn't intrude: My favorite CDs are the boys' choir recorded in the Basilica of Montserrat; the Balla Tounkara, ancient music performed on a solo acoustic kora, the West African harp; Debussy's *La mer;* Mozart's strings— the more Zen-like the atmosphere the better.

The mind should be suspended. Go where the music takes you. Revisiting sexual highlights of the past is not a good place to go nor are the problems and worries of the day. A fantasy of clouds, the ocean, idyllic meadows, birds in flight, that's the ticket. Once your mind surrenders to the clarity and sweetness of the nap, a unique tranquility overcomes you, all the threats and terrors that assail your night sleep are banished, and the nap performs as a short refresher that enhances the resumed hours of the day and evening thanks to the alchemy of sleep, marvelously extolled by Don Quixote: "Now, blessings light on him that first invented this same sleep! It covers a man all over, thoughts and all, like a cloak; it is meat for the hungry, drink for the thirsty, heat for the cold, and cold for the hot. It is the current coin that purchases all the pleasures of the world cheap; and the balance that sets the king and the shepherd, the fool and the wise man even."

What time to take a daily nap cannot be arbitrary—plunking yourself down when the time is convenient can only work if that time coincides with your diurnal dip. Years ago, I wrote about Duke University's sleep research department, and that is how I discovered the diurnal curve that is a barometer of an individual's highs and lows of energy as indicated by his temperature. An individual's diurnal curve is determined from a succession of hourly temperature readings from morning until night. When your temperature is high, your energy is high, but then it gradually descends to its lowest point, which is when your energy has bottomed out—that is precisely when a nap is in order. Individuals hit their highs and lows at varying times, but it is consistent in each person. As a result of my hourly temperature readings, I found that my optimum naptime was when my temperature dipped to its lowest point, around 3:45. I had always felt a kind of fatigue at that time that I had tried to overcome with strong coffee or a spin on the treadmill or both but neither, I discovered, came close to the restoration of a nap.

As I write this it's ten to four, I'm running out of juice, so this is a good time to sign off and stretch out on my favorite chaise while L'Escolania Boys Choir sings the Montserrat hymn, "The Vivolai."

First you forget names, then you forget faces,
then you forget to pull your zipper up,
then you forget to pull your zipper down.

—ANONYMOUS

What You Can't Hear
Can't Hurt You

———

Of all the trying conundrums an elderly party has to solve, one of the most trying is when to surrender to the stigma of displaying a hearing aid. I say stigma because there it is for all the world to see, this advertisement of one's dissembling. Not as trying for the ladies who camouflage the telltale bugs with their flowing locks, but a public revelation for the gents who might as well announce, "People, I am starting to go downhill."

So every effort is made to postpone putting that humiliating bug in one's ear. In fact, it takes quite a while for one even to realize that one's hearing is tuning out, quite like it was when one slowly came to realize that it wasn't that the lights were dim, it was a need for an initial pair of reading glasses. So it is that at first one accusingly asks people not to mumble, to speak up; one gradually increases the television volume; one plugs one's free ear with one's finger when one is on the phone; one is annoyed with movies that have characters who don't "project," especially in the whispered love scenes, or while they are planning, sotto voce, when to jump the bad guy. "In my day," one says, "with John Wayne, Bette Davis, Katie Hepburn you heard every word."

A member of the family is usually the one who comes right out and tells you that maybe you should check your hearing. Your doctor checks you and you are shocked to discover that you are borderline and you could use a little aural help. But you continue to resist, until you watch a John Wayne movie on the Turner Classic Movies channel and, sadly, the Duke is mumbling like the rest of them.

Now you contact friends who have hearing aids for advice and you're subjected to a series of horror stories. Too much background noise. Sudden surges of volume. Buzzing sounds. Screeches. Headaches. A really good one will empty your bank account.

You soldier on, trying to read lips, straining to pick up tailing sentences, trying not to sound cranky when you say, "What's that?" or, "What'd you say?" or, "Huh?"

Eventually you capitulate, as you did when you finally put on a knee elastic for tennis. You go to the hearing place the doctor recommends. They put you through a regimen of trials and errors, trying this one and that one. On one device you are listening to two aliens having a quarrel. Another trial aid shrieks every time you pass a certain electronic grid. Another wavers in and out.

Then one day they get it right. No one has to shout any more, and when you go to the movies you hear everything, even when, in a bad movie, bombs bursting around them, the young lovers cling to each other and whisper their eternal devotion. Moments like that make you nostalgic for the good "old" days, when, without your hearing aid, you couldn't hear them.

Sometimes the hearing aid may lead to unintended consequences. A man I know, Norbert by name, who is a certified electronic wizard, provided himself with an unexpected bonus when he finally capitulated and acquired a high-end hearing aid. Norbert decided that if he had to tolerate this loathsome contrivance in his ear, he would have some fun with it. With his electronic wizardry, he created a tiny wireless receptor that he could hide in the palm of his hand and capture conversation, the receptor automatically transmitting the conversation to his hearing aid.

His inquisitive hidden receptor put all conversation in jeopardy, especially that of those who thought their gossip was private. At dinner parties he could hear what the couple across the table was cattily confiding to each other about people at the table, including himself.

Norbert kept his sly invention secret but eventually it gave him an unexpected shock when it picked up his wife confiding to her seating partner how dreadfully Norbert treated her and how she planned to leave him.

Their subsequent confrontation wasn't pretty, but eventually Norbert and his wife happily resolved their grievances. As part of their reconstructed togetherness, Norbert was obliged to scrap his eavesdropping.

Your Stockpiling Years
Are Now Paying Dividends

Once you motor past the seventy-year marker, you become a recipient of these privileges and indulgences:

- dozing at inappropriate times;
- forgetting appointments, birthdays, anniversaries, names, etc.;
- belching and farting;
- exhibiting eccentricity;
- using scatological words and raunchy jokes;
- cutting in on lines at banks, bus stops, taxi stands, etc.;
- criticizing under the camouflage of wisdom;
- outrageous lying, masquerading as exaggeration;
- zigzagging political convictions;
- pinching samples from fruit stands and bakeries;

- asking someone to snatch your bag from the airport carousel as it goes by;
- talking to yourself out loud;
- giving tips that diminish in proportion to increasing age;
- as waistlines broaden, tailors and seamstresses keep pace;
- borrowing from relatives;
- foregoing colonoscopies, as intestines now deemed too brittle.

SUNG AT AN AARP EVENT

Maalox and nose drops and needles for knitting,
Walkers and handrails and new dental fittings,
Bundles of magazines tied up in strings,
These are a few of my favorite things.

Cadillacs and cataracts, hearing aids and glasses,
Polident and Fixodent and false teeth in glasses,
Pacemakers, golf carts and porches with swings,
These are a few of my favorite things.

When the pipes leak, when the bones creak,
When the knees go bad,
I simply remember my favorite things,
And then I don't feel so sad.

Hot tea and crumpets and corn pads for bunions,
No spicy hot food or food cooked with onions,
Bathrobes and heating pads and hot meals they bring,
These are a few of my favorite things.

Back pains, confused brains, and no need for sinnin',
Thin bones and fractures and hair that is thinnin',
And we won't mention our short shrunken frames,
When we remember our favorite things.

When the joints ache, when the hips break,
When the eyes grow dim,
Then I remember the great life I've had,
And then I don't feel so bad.

—Anonymous

Nip Your Nuptial Before
Your Nuptial Nips You

You may think that upon reaching the age of enlighten-
ment, having made their peace with past marital tribulations, like divorce and spousal loss, super seniors would
abide their placid status. But no, like many other nonagenarians, he eighty-nine, she ninety or vice versa, they are
pledging themselves to holy matrimony at a festive ceremony arranged at the assisted living facility where they
met and fell in love.

Marriage among the chronologically challenged has
steadily increased, leaving gerontologists to ponder why
seniors who fall in love, once content simply to live together,
are now stapling themselves to a marriage license with all its
myriad implications for property ownership, will provisions,
taxes, life insurance, and all the rest. Your house or mine?
Your car or my car or both? Who drives? Whose furniture?

A budget? Assets? Expenses? Stocks, bonds, etcetera, shared or separate?

Subscribers to the Internet's SeniorPeopleMeet, which claims over 700,000 active members in the upper ages, find what the Web site calls their "mature match," and often, ignoring the advice of their children, obtain marriage licenses and exchange rings, the children having to cope with the specter of their eighty-nine-year-old father with a rose pinned to his lapel, exchanging vows with a slightly older lady with a gardenia corsage on her wrist. The children had been looking after pop since mom passed on, but now they have been pushed aside, faced with having to assimilate their new supergenarian mother-in-law into their married lives. They are also privately concerned about how pop's acquisition of this mother-in-law will affect their inheritances.

All these problems are minor, however, compared to the ones that spring up when the newlyweds, set in their ways, find that the demands of matrimony are more than they can handle. Compromise does not come easily to an eighty-nine-year-old who has been living alone for ten years. The senior couple may solve their split amicably, but more often than not, heated squabbles force the children back into action, sometimes with lawyers, his children doing battle with her children.

That's the situation my friend, Stuart, had to face. "At the beginning of his marriage, we didn't see Dad very often, but then he started to come around more frequently, without her, and less than a year into his marriage, he moved out of the apartment, which had been hers. Dad had given up his condo.

"When it came to divvying up their assets, it was a nightmare, each one claiming the things the other one claimed. Her children thought he was out of line and hired a lawyer, and we felt the same way and hired our own lawyer. It was the items they had acquired together that caused the rumble. Like, Annie, the Siamese kitten they had obtained from the local pet store, the dining room set, the wedding presents.

"Dad got depressed and isolated himself in a rented studio. I almost got into a fistfight with one of her sons. My sisters and my wife had done everything we could to stop him from marrying her, but now we had to mop up the nasty consequences. Dad's now living with us."

Attorney Ed Weidenfeld, a veteran of these dustups, says, "These court battles go on interminably and turn into a psychodrama that is a Who did Daddy love most? Me or the wicked witch he married after mother? I've seen kids absolutely devastated by not having expectations met."

From personal experience I know what he means. Back in my brief lawyer days, I encountered a few combative heirs, like the one who was incensed that Daddy had willed to his late-acquired wife what he had promised to her.

"I can't believe he left her the house."

"The will is quite specific that—"

"The will! There was—what do you call it?"

"Undue influence."

"You're damn right! Lots of undue influence. He would never in a million years have left anything to that bitch."

"I think it would be best if we could discuss this—"

"He was ninety-one years old—can't you claim he wasn't in his right mind? He must have been crazy leaving the house to an old bitch like that. She's what? Eighty-eight? Now she has it in her will. So how long will she last? She wheezes. A year maybe. Then it goes to her loathsome son. My house! The son'll sleep in my bed with that snaggle-toothed wife of his!"

"But you haven't lived in that house for twenty—"

"But I would have if he'd have left it to me. That's what he always said. 'Wizzy-woozums' . . . that's what he called me since I was a toddler. 'Wizzy-woozums, you and your kids will be living here some day,' Hah!"

"She's still your stepmother, you know. You can visit—"

"That'll be the day!"

"Your dad did leave you the Mercedes and the—"

"She has bad breath."

". . . Warhols."

". . . and she has a filthy temper. She once called me a spoiled brat. Brat! I'm sixty years old, to be treated like this! Daddy would never in his right mind leave the house to an old bitch with false teeth. How many times he said, 'Wizzy-woozums, you and your kids—'"

"You already said that."

"Then, okay, gear up! Let's sue her ass off! He was mentally, uh, didn't know what he was doing."

"That would be hard to prove."

"Why? Their word—oh, that greedy son of hers and that kvetching wife of his!—against mine."

"Just before his heart attack, your father had made a brilliant speech before the Rotary Club. It would be hard to prove he was of unsound mind."

"I'm telling you now, I'm gonna burn the house down before she gets to move in."

"All right. I just want you to know, I don't handle arson cases."

The dissolution may be especially combative when one of the spouses is considerably older than the other, as was the case, for example, when the marriage of twenty-seven-year-old Anna Nicole Smith, a curvaceous Marilyn Monroe look-alike, to an eighty-nine-year-old oil tycoon, J. Howard Marshall II, came to an abrupt end. Anna Nicole was a topless dancer in a strip club where she caught the eye of Marshall, the owner of the Great Northern Oil Company. They married in 1994 and he died a year later, indicating that a year of Anna Nicole in the marital bed was a bit more than J. Howard could handle. His demise precipitated a fierce battle between Anna Nicole and her stepson, E. Pierce Marshall.

A California court awarded Anna $474 million but that

award was overturned on appeal; the court, however, granting her the right to a new trial. But the untimely death of the stepson at age sixty-seven complicated the lawsuit that was further complicated by the precipitous death of Anna Nicole at age thirty-seven, probably ending the litigation.

It is not only sugar daddies who get into this kind of tangle, but there are also sugar mommies who marry much younger men who sometimes have grandmothers younger than their bride. These marriages may run into trouble when the young husband wants to be a father but the "mature" wife can no longer oblige.

I am muddying these marital waters in order to demonstrate that there is a raft that can keep some divorcing seniors afloat while others around them are sinking. The name of the raft is: PRENUPTIAL. Before the lapel rose and the wrist gardenia, super seniors should write down what is relevant about their assets, children, trusts, those concerns unique to the elderly. There are prenups that even specify finite details like who does the cooking, who cleans up, his ration of sports on television, who pays the bills, how frequently they have sex (once a month is popular), who does the shopping, who goes to the cleaners.

There are lawyers who specialize in drafting prenups for seniors and you can find them on the Internet where they have posted lengthy articles about prenuptials. To be sure a prenup is properly prepared it is probably best to consult one of these lawyers who specialize in family law.

J. Howard could have protected his estate from its tribulations with Anna Nicole if he had executed a prenup that provided terms based on the length of their marriage. Matrimonial lawyers have a standard schedule that determines what the wealthier spouse has to pay from his/her individual bank account:

marriage of less than one year: $100,000;
marriage of more than one but less than two years: $200,000;
marriage of more than two years: $300,000.

Of course these amounts are adjustable, but depending on whether the young spouse-to-be agrees or refuses to sign on, it is a solid clue as to whether he/she is marrying for love or for money. This ruling by the Florida Court of Appeals demonstrates how a signed prenup has its merits:

This appeal evolves from the divorce of an elderly, wealthy furniture magnate after less than three years of marriage to his much younger wife. We have no quarrel with the conclusion of the trial judge that the wife is not entitled to a $150,000 Rolls-Royce. She will just have to be content with her Cadillac, gifts of jewelry in excess of $150,000 and the $700,000 in cash bestowed on her by the prenuptial agreement.

So, a final word to senior spouses-to-be: Don't neglect to put your Rolls-Royce in your prenup.

Although the prenup is an effective catch basin for identifying who owns what before the marital knot gets tied, it does not encompass what the superannuated couple acquires after they are Mr. and Mrs., and that's what leads to all the squabbling if the late-blooming union wilts. I think it's unfortunate that divvying up these mutually acquired possessions is taken seriously, with families and lawyers becoming involved.

Why not solve the dissolution in the same light-hearted way the couple plighted their troth? Why not a wheel of fortune that puts all the disputed possessions in the categories of the wheel? The disillusioned couple take turns spinning the wheel, and the spinner gets what the wheel stops on. Husband's spin lands on the new toaster oven, that's his. The wife's spin hits the DVD player, it goes with her.

To paraphrase a bit, life is a carnival, dear chum, we took a chance marrying at eighty-eight, why not a wheel of chance when we're dividing up at ninety?

Fortunately, most often the marriage of the two old parties succeeds and they have a fine time during their carnival years, playing life's wheel of fortune together.

Between the years of ninety-two to a hundred and two . . . we shall be the ribald, useless drunken outcast person we have always wished to be. We shall have a long white beard and long white hair; we shall not walk at all, but recline in a wheel chair and bellow for alcoholic beverages; in the winter we shall sit before the fire with our feet in a bucket of hot water, with a decanter of corn whiskey near at hand, and write ribald songs against organized society; strapped to one arm of our chair will be a forty-five caliber revolver, and we shall shoot out the lights when we want to go to sleep, instead of turning them off; when we want air we shall toss a silver candlestick through the front window and be damned to it; we shall address public meetings to which we have been invited because of our wisdom in a vein of jocund malice. But we don't wish to make any one envious of the good time that is coming to us . . . we look forward to a disreputable, vigorous, unhonored and disorderly old age.

— *Don Marquis,* "The Almost Perfect State"

Yes, Richard,
There Is a Santa Claus

When I invited my old friend Richard to lunch to celebrate his ninetieth birthday, I knew, from the way he sounded on the phone, that it would be more than just our usual lunch at Moriarity's. Not that anything about Richard is usual. I have been friends with him longer than anyone, and I have become accustomed to the peaks and valleys of his idiosyncrasies.

We originally met at the start of World War II at the huge Air Force induction center at Sheppard Field, Texas, Richard from the Bronx, me from St Louis. I had been detached from duty, performing in an Air Force musical I co-wrote that we GIs performed in nearby Wichita Falls, and Richard was one of those GIs. Later, when General Fickle sent us on tour (yes, that was his real name), Richard and I became solid buddies.

After the tour, each of us now second lieutenants, we were

sent to different theaters of war, but we renewed our friend-ship when I moved to New York after the war ended. Rich-ard had returned to his place in the Bronx and he has remained faithful to the Bronx ever since. He married when he has twenty-nine, but when they had a baby a year later, he made it clear that he was extending the custom in the Air Force—officers do not carry packages, umbrellas, or newspapers—to include diapering, feeding, or pushing a baby buggy. When his wife, Rachel, insisted that he move to Roslyn, Long Island, for the baby's sake (her awful parents lived a block away), Richard vowed he'd never leave the Bronx and that was that.

After the divorce, Richard never married again. He fancied himself an inventor in the mold of Edison and Alexander Graham Bell, but reality did not accompany his fancy. To sup-port himself he worked a variety of jobs, including working on an assembly line at a company that made shopping bags.

Although he was fired from that job, Richard stumbled onto a way to make a better handle, obtained a patent, and in no time company after company (including the one that fired him) were paying him steady royalties to use his patent.

Richard became wealthy and was quite generous and happy with his largesse, but on the occasion of this lunch, he had something of importance on his mid.

"It's my ninetieth," he said, "so I figured it was time to take stock where I'm going."

"Where have you got in mind?"

"No, not a trip, where I'm going."

"Where's that?"

"You know how some people, they've got dual passports?"

"I thought you'd never move from the Bronx."

"Not the Bronx. I mean, now that I'm ninety, it's time to think about the hereafter. I want two men of God to help me out."

"What men of God?"

"You know I'm already Jewish, but I'd like two shots at the hereafter so I'm going Catholic, too. I figure with a rabbi and a priest taking care of me, I've got twice as good a chance to wind up in a very nice place. So there's this Catholic Church in my neighborhood where I went to the confessional, sat down and told the priest I wanted to join up."

"Just like that?"

"He asked if I had been baptized and I said Jews don't baptize, but I'd be willing."

"You'd really get baptized?"

"Sure, what's a little water?"

"Did you ask him if you'd have to give up being Jewish?"

"Naw, he didn't ask. I've been meeting him regularly in his rectory. We've become good friends. Listen, I like being a part-time Catholic. Not the same as being a Jew all my life, but I've been working at it. I've studied, really I have. I've done the catechumen and all the other stuff."

"You go to mass?"

"Of course. I love all the pageantry. I've done Lent, and I've done Easter Vigil."

"And were you baptized?"

"Oh, yes. Listen, I'm really into this."

"And you still go to synagogue?"

"Of course. The high holidays, the minyans, Passover, the whole lot. I'm just as Jewish as I ever was."

"So you go back and forth from Hanukah to Christmas?"

"Yeah, but the funny thing is I seem to screw up some of the Christmas carols." He ordered another round of Jameson's. "Rabbi Meyers and Father Terrence are good friends now. We sometimes have a drink together."

"All three of you?"

"Don't be dumb! I mean I'm Jewish with the rabbi and Catholic with Father Terrence."

"But who gets the most allegiance? I see you have an enameled Christmas tree pinned on your lapel."

"Tomorrow it gets replaced," he said, turning up his lapel to reveal a Star of David on the other side "Can you imagine what a send-off I'll get? Nobody can get out of this world alone but I'm in very good shape."

*Like all great travelers,
I have seen more than I remember,
and remember more than I have seen.*
—BENJAMIN DISRAELI

The World Is Your Oyster,
So Shuck It

~

Our country was founded and populated by peripatetic forefathers whose travel bloodlines have run through the veins of their descendants—which accounts for the massive cruise ships that ferry the population of the United States around the world's oceans. College graduates take a year or two "off" to see the world. Honeymooners celebrate their togetherness in romantic settings in faraway places. Retirees see what they might have missed.

My own immediate predecessors came from Hungary and Poland; true to his nomad inheritance, my father, who emigrated from Kraków, was a traveling salesman, covering the Midwest, and my maternal grandfather, from Budapest, gypsied his family around the United States, my mother included, opening Hungarian restaurants in one city after another, St. Louis to Oklahoma City to Chicago to Milwaukee, moving just in time to avoid the authorities.

I have inherited this peripatetic strain. I have had a flat in London; a house in Honfleur, Normandy; an apartment in Trouville, France; three apartments in Paris over the years, on the Boulevard Saint-Germain, rue de Berri, and the Boulevard Monceau, opposite the Parc Monceau where my son attended school; Rome where I rented the apartment of an indigent *principesa* (aren't they all?) on the Viale di Villa Massimo; a pensione flat at Lago di Garda in Italy. Add to that my four years in the air force stationed in various places, and, afterward, in domestic cities like Hollywood and Wellfleet, Massachusetts.

The urge to travel often increases with age, as if time might limit the number of places one can check off on one's wish list. By the time you reach eighty and beyond, if you have not yet cracked your passport, in your eagerness to make up for lost time you may overreach with depressing results. There are nonagenarians who have never set foot beyond their native habitats but who, with their years counting down, want to make amends and finally put on their traveling shoes. Berlitz has made a fortune teaching these late-blooming American tourists, intent on revisiting their ancestral beginnings, to speak foreign languages badly. If these tourists try to make up for lost time and do too much, or take on an itinerary that is unsuitable, they may wind up bitterly disappointed instead of enjoying their delayed sabbatical.

When my mother was eighty-three, she decided, along

with a close friend, to take her first trip abroad. She was in good shape, fiercely independent, drove her vintage Chevy to work every day, and so eagerly anticipated her first trip to Europe, arranged by a local travel agent. My mother had had a hard life struggling to help our family survive the Great Depression, at the same time struggling to overcome recurring tuberculosis. She had lived alone since my father died and methodically set aside travel funds from her salary. She outfitted herself with luggage, new clothes, guidebooks.

But the two weeks abroad she had so eagerly anticipated turned out to be an exasperating experience. In those fourteen days her tour bus stopped in twelve different cities, twelve different hotels, my mother packing and unpacking every day, prearranged meals in prearranged restaurants where the succulent dinners going by them to regular diners bore no resemblance to the fare on their plates. When she returned, my mother told me that the hectic schedule had not given her time to sort out what she saw; her memory of her trip was just a jumble of inchoate impressions.

Travel agents who book elderly people on quick and easy tours like that should be run over by the tour bus, but fortunately there are a predominant number of responsible agents who do arrange itineraries suited to the traveler's advanced age, his psyche and his pocketbook.

Which brings us to the preferred travel today: giant cruise ships that are floating hotels, as big and busy as the New

York Hilton, less than ideal for an eighty-five-year-old couple that wanted to enjoy the quiet of the sea. These monster ships' virtue is that once on board you unpack and don't repack until you return to homeport. But on entering your stateroom, before unpacking, you have an initial jolt trying to equate your cramped accommodation with the picture the travel agent had shown you in the brochure. There are four or five restaurants of different cuisines (Red Lobster quality), open seating (which means no reservations, catch as catch can), several swimming pools with splashing youngsters, a number of movie screens showing movies you don't want to see, a casino, a spa (extra charge), a discotheque, lots of noisy activity all over the decks. I have just received a brochure from one of the major cruise companies, Oceania, whose ships plow the world's oceans and seas. Looking at those schedules, I'm reminded of my mother's unhappy trip. The ten-day voyage from Athens to Rome, for example, puts in at ten different ports in Turkey, Greece, and Italy for a few hours every day. You eat moussaka for dinner in Athens and brush your teeth in Rome.

There are smaller cruise ships, better suited to nonagenarians, as well as trips down the Danube and the canals of France, which a good travel agent can arrange. And he would steer you clear of the Club Meds and other undesirable locations for super seniors.

I myself have avoided modern cruise ships. Long ago I crossed the oceans on the Queens, *Mary* and *Elizabeth,* the

Ile de France, and the *Constitution,* but those were quiet and elegant days at sea at a different time.

Whether by sea, bus, or train, with or without a good guide, a visit to any of the touted sights abroad, be it the Louvre, the Colosseum, or Buckingham Palace, alumni tours to the Incas and St. Petersburg, these trips consist of viewing cliché sights that are monuments to the past, perfectly satisfying if you want everything sound and prearranged.

But if you still have spirit within you for real adventure, I have found two modes that I think adventurous nonagenarians would relish. The first is to swap your dwelling for the dwelling of your counterpart across the United States or in a foreign country. An eighty-year-old couple I know swapped their Santa Monica digs last year for a place in Paris and they are still enthusing over the experience. I have swapped my Connecticut house several times for places in Rome, Normandy, and Paris, and I can tell you that when you reside in a foreign locale and you are not a tourist, your experience is much more agreeable. Life is less expensive and language is not a problem—my high school French improved during my stay in Paris and the Romans were encouraging as I learned to speak ungrammatical Italian. The thrill of shopping for dinner among the food stalls and carts on a Paris street, or going down to the docks in Honfleur to view the fish as the trawlers unload their catches, or dining on squid and pasta at a little trattoria in Trastevere, this has the unique appeal of being involved in the life of those cities.

To facilitate such exchanges, there are Web sites that require a small entry fee and provide reliable access to desirable places that will give you a refreshing change of living without much expenditure except for your travel. The swap can even include automobiles.

Adventurous as a swapped home may be, there is a vacation that without doubt, is the most exciting and most enjoyable I have ever experienced—the safari. What! For super seniors? Yes, indeed. I went on my first safari when I was eighty-eight, and my second the year after. I am thinking of going a third time next year. Of all the places I've been—and as I've demonstrated I've been to many of the most desirable—the safari is the only time I felt that I was participating in true life as it was evolving, life of unexpected surprises and revelations, a primitive life beautiful and brutal, a life that infused me with its life.

Good safaris are made to your order. Where you go, what you do, how you do it, how much it costs, is up to you. Bush pilots, who land their little planes on dirt strips, took Virginia and me to safari camps in Botswana, Malawi, Namibia, Tanzania, Zambia, and Zimbabwe, each camp with distinct characteristics of animals, terrain, vegetation, birds, big and little fauna, and exotic flora. If this sounds like it's too vigorous for the nonagenarian, I can assure you it is not. The head of Africa Calls in Phoenix, Arizona, who arranged both our safaris, told me that last year they sent a group of four ninety-four-year-olds, one of whom walked with a cane, on a safari that was completely successful. Your age and mobility dictate where you go and how you go but wherever you go, you are seated in a safari vehicle that takes you everywhere, right up to and sometimes among the animals and the unique vegetation. You may closely follow two lionesses as they stalk a kudu and chase it down, sharing it for dinner.

No two camps are alike in their situs, their physicality, and their typography. We wanted to start with a primitive camp, like the ones in the early Hemingway days when there were white hunters and gun bearers. So our first camp was very small—three screened tents with no running water (showers by appointment with river water released from an overhead drum), illumination by candles and kerosene lamps. The camp is run by an outstanding naturalist, Phil Berry, and his wife, Babette. In the night, herds of water buffalo passed by our screens and hippos munched on the grass nearby. Subsequent camps on our safari were more substantial and located on the banks of rivers and lakes, on plains and the fringe of forests. The Sausage Tree Camp in Zambia is named for their tree pods as big as salamis that hang from branches and we watched elephants harvest them with their elevated trunks. In all the camps, elephants, buffalos, lions, hyenas, and hippos roamed the campgrounds at night, without incident, but armed guards were there just in case.

My diary notations tell the story:

- a daisy chain of eighty-five elephants with babies are crossing the river, tails to trunks;
- family of baboons splashing on the riverbank;
- leopard with captured mongoose snatched away from him by a hyena. Another leopard appears with a small kill that he carries up an acacia tree to feed to two babies hidden in a fork in the branches;
- the tantalizing smell of Africa, like no other, sandalwood combined with the pungent aromas of wild sage, wild basil, and divine lavender;
- bathrooms are open to the sky. A monkey drops in and watches me shave. I must keep my razor in a secure drawer or when I come back from today's trip, I might find him in front of my mirror shaving with my razor;
- ninety-five hippos packed together in a shallow of water, their sound a symphony of tubas;
- a herd of gnus, crossword puzzle come to life;
- a walking safari with Phil Berry observing incredible variety of birds, a Lilac-breasted Roller doing cartwheels right over our heads;
- we are on a night drive—wild dogs in the headlights, running down an impala, their faces covered with its blood, set upon by hyenas, one big female, three males, brief furious fight, dogs driven away by the hyenas. Female hyena keeps males at bay while she eats the impala, bones and all. Our Land

Rover follows her while she is moving the carcass. One male grabs a leg that drops but that's all they get;

- a tree covered with green and red parrots;
- spectacular start today. Lionesses have just killed and torn open a zebra, then four huge males move in, chase them and their seventeen cubs away, ferocious chorus of growls, earth shakes, as the males tear the carcass apart, cubs try to get in, swatted away by the males, lionesses patiently await their turn, cubs keep trying, as males tear flesh from the bones, sound diminishes, cubs get a little bit but lionesses defer, a roaring tableau;
- we make many attempts to locate a rhino but they are almost extinct due to vicious poaching. Finally there he is, body armor, square jaw, enormous, follow him as he grazes. Only six known to be in area;
- a confluence of giraffes. Count eighteen. Two giraffes, male and female, thirty feet away from us, in an incredible mating dance. Rubbing their necks, coiling their necks around each other, moving to a rhythm, a delicate dance that calls for *Swan Lake* music;
- the food in the camps is superlative—gather around the log fire outside (the temperature drops at night), and enjoy the breathtaking sky with its

dense canopy of stars. It's as if all the skies of the universe have emptied their stars into the African sky above us and they are hanging so low you think you can reach up and pick them like figs.

The last leg of our second safari topped them all. We are with a group of eleven on this trip, led by Richard, one of Africa's best guides. Ages of the group from seventies to eighties. We fly to Lake Tanganyika, the second largest, deepest freshwater lake in the world, bordered by a huge dense tropical forest. Rising above are the Mahale Mountains, home to the world's largest population of chimpanzees. We transfer from our plane to an old scow that looks like the *African Queen*'s sister, but without Humphrey Bogart. The scow chugs along for an hour when suddenly there is a surprising clearing in the dense forest and the remarkable Greystoke Mahale appears at the foot of the mountain. The exotic wooden bandas on the white sand beach are open fronted and fashioned from dhow timber. Our destination, a family of sixty chimps that lies within hiking distance. The following morning we follow a guide on a steep trail up the mountain to meet the chimps. I am all right with the climb but a little bothered by the increasingly thin mountain air. The chimps are busy with their lives when we emerge. Mothers with their babies. Little chimps playing games in the branches. Darwin, a huge male who is the mayor, comes barreling down the path, brushing us aside.

The chimps, all of them named by the guides, are accustomed to human presence so we are all right in their "house." All the people in our group are busy with their cameras, except me. I use my eyes and memory as my camera. I am sitting alone, when a large male comes out of the forest, comes over to me, gives me a close squinted look—a look I had seen many times when I was a boy selling periodicals door to door—then with a wave of his hand he continues on his way. I learned his name was Christmas and he was considered the resident comedian.

With all these options—from a cruise to a safari—the nonagenarian who is reasonably fit in body and pocket, should shake himself from senior lethargy and douse himself with the elixir of travel. I can't guarantee Darwin or Christmas will greet you in the Mahale Mountains, but I give you fair warning that if you opt for a sedentary life in front of television, you may wake up some day and find moss growing on your backside.

From the letters, which I wrote at that period [my youth],
I plainly see that we have certain advantages and
disadvantages at every time of life, as compared
with earlier or later periods.
Thus, in my fortieth year, I was as clear
and decided on some subjects as at present,
and in many respects superior to my present self
yet now, in my eightieth,
I possess advantages which I should not like
to exchange for those.

—GOETHE

When You Leave What You Leave, Do You Leave It?

_~_

When I was in law school, "intestate" was one of our casebooks' scurrilous words. The professor who lectured on the subject told us about a freshman student who, on first encountering the word, thought it referred to undescended testicles. What intestate does refer to is a person who dies without leaving a will; what he does leave is a mess. Although the deceased may have nothing much to bequest, and only one obvious person to inherit it, it may be a mess because of another scurrilous word: "contestants."

Even when there is a will, those left out can challenge it with attack-dog lawyers, but in most cases a proper will wins out. It is puzzling, therefore, why so many elders die intestate. They probably regard executing the will as a costly procedure that can be put off for the time being: "After all I have a long time till I'm dead, ha ha!" How often the assets of an intestate are expended in litigation over who's entitled to what. If only the deceased had realized that in most states any procrastinating senior, like himself, can execute an instant will: Just take pen and paper and write, "I leave all my worldly goods to my wife, Emma." Date it and sign it and get two bowling buddies to sign as witnesses to your signature and voilà, a will! The courts are so anxious to validate wills they have even recognized a simple sentence written for an illiterate who signed with an "X."

But there's no need to be circumspect. If you suffer from ATL (Aversion To Lawyers), it is possible to buy the form of a simple will at your stationers or perhaps on the Internet and record the relevant entries. You cannot be sure, however, that there are not conditions in your bequeathal that should be addressed by an attorney. Even though I practiced law back in the Middle Ages, I know better than to trust my rusting recall with writing my own will. I knew an attorney who specializes in wills and estates and he drew a will that encompasses some provisions I probably would have overlooked. One of those provisions, for example, was that if anyone mentioned in the will contests any of its bequeathal, that person will be excommunicated from the will with a bequeathal of one dollar.

I guess you have divined by now that I am strongly in favor of (1) leaving the world testate; (2) creating a proper will; (3) having a lawyer do it; (4) discouraging challenges as much as possible.

There is one procedure, related to the will, that carries

the most potential for nasty squabbling—the division of personal possessions. The contents of every room in your house, items in the garage, your car(s), jewelry, the tool shed, your pets, luggage, furniture, clothes, silverware, etcetera, ought to be allocated. During the brief time I practiced law, as a rookie barrister in the firm of Taylor Mayer Shifrin & Willer, I was assigned squabbles related to divorces, wills, common law bust-ups, and the like. There was the case of the brother and sister, sole inheritors, who had amicably agreed on how to divvy the house, cars, time-share, stocks, but they were at each other over who got the pet canary. I suggested a revolving six months' share but they refused because Mellifluous became depressed and stopped singing if he traveled. That case was solved when Mellifluous, probably depressed by the squabbling of the inheritors, somehow escaped his cage and flew away, never to be seen again. I had another case where twin brothers who had amicably worked out co-ownership of the beer company their father had left them, ceased talking and cross-litigated because they both wanted their father's vintage beer mug collection.

At a particularly nasty session in my office, I was inspired to come up with a solution: a boyhood pal of mine, Jason Rivers, ran a bar on the St. Louis waterfront. I suggested we meet there and the brothers could duel it out with steins of beer rather than litigious swords.

Jason put three steins of his special beer in front of each brother. At my command, they were to drink the beers as fast as they could; the one who drained all three before the other would get the collection. The furiously sudsy competition ended in a dead tie, both of them banging down their number three mugs at the same moment. The brothers threw their arms around each other, embraced, and spent the rest of the night lowering Jason's supply of his special brew. They cheerfully agreed to take turns choosing from the collection.

Silly squabbles, I had learned, deserve silly solutions.

There's a good way to stifle this kind of niggling combat among inheritors: I have inventoried every item of value in every room in the house, designating precisely who gets what, from the piano to the paintings on the wall to the crystal vases and the treadmill. I attached this inventory to my will. My attorney tells me that this kind of inventory has virtually eliminated inheritor squabbles. (And yes, my parrot Ernie is in there.)

But there is one thing about a will that cannot be expunged—resentment toward the deceased by an inheritor because of a perceived slight in the distribution of the will's goodies. I refer to that august occasion when the lawyer assembles all the inheritors in his office for a reading of the will, who gets what and who doesn't, a dramatic moment often mined by playwrights. These occasions are sometimes punctuated with cries of outrage and denunciation, but fortunately you are now ensconced on high and only hearing the swinging band of heavenly harps led by Benny Goodman.

*They say the first thing to go when you're old
is your legs or your eyesight. It isn't true.
The first thing to go is parallel parking.*

—KURT VONNEGUT

It's All Hanging
in the Balance

~~~~~~

The physical threats that increase as one's age increases affect nonagenarians in one of two ways: There are the alarmists and there are the deniers. The alarmists react to every new ache and pain as warnings of dire developments in their bodies and they rush to their doctors with their inflamed fears, expecting the doctors to confirm the anticipated bad news. The deniers, on the other hand, disregard these alleged symptoms, sometimes regrettably, and steer clear of doctors until they believe they are necessary. They are a boon for Medicare. They also have a more pleasurable existence than the introspective alarmists.

As the shadows of advancing years fall upon both camps, they bring with them one troublesome condition that the alarmists' doctors cannot deny, nor can the deniers disregard: balance. No matter how sound your body, how stable your legs, how clear your mind, they do not spare you from imbalance, especially when navigating stairs. There are medical explanations for this phenomenon but they don't offer any help except to "be careful," which is no solace. How many times do we read obits of elderly people whose demise was caused by a fall, often in their homes. My friend Kurt Vonnegut's life ended that way. Even if a fall is not lethal it can result in physical damage: A fractured pelvis takes a long time to heal.

Balance is one instance where both camps embrace the same support: canes. To give them cachet, some deniers call them "walking sticks," à la the Brits, and decorate the handles, but canes or walking sticks they are a wobbly senior's best friend as they are for seniors with gimpy knees. Jaunty deniers use their walking sticks with flair, giving their appearance a certain *je ne sais quoi* look, suggesting that they are Fred Astaire, about to break out in a paroxysm of cane tapping at any moment.

But there's a challenge that needs more than a cane—negotiating stairs. I live in an old three-story house, my study on the top floor. The stairs are long and winding and I have slipped several times on stairs that are not well lit. Recently, however, I received a very welcome gift from a man who was pleased with one of my books and knowing my age, sent me an invention of his (available on the Internet) that he thought would be useful. It's a small compact light powered by batteries that is designed for stairs; it illuminates several steps above and below it and is activated automatically when the person approaches its position on the stairwell and deactivates when the person leaves its vicinity. I have put them at intervals on the stairs. Mr. Beam, it is regrettably called, but it has facilitated my ups and downs nicely.

Some of my friends have found a drastic solution to the stairs menace by giving up their houses and moving to stairless condominiums and one-level ranches. Not me. I have lived and worked in this Normandy-style house since 1954. The stripling white birches I planted along the long winding approach to the house are now towering guardians that have interwoven their branches and formed a lovely bower all along the driveway. The other trees and bushes I planted, the gazebo my young son helped erect twenty-five years ago, the reflecting pool with its fountain and family of koi, the rock dens where the chipmunks and the resident woodchuck live, the hen house with its complement of pedigreed beauties, adjoined by a pen of Royal Blue Peacocks, the trellises of roses and firethorns, the flowering crabapple, the weeping cherry—this wonderful world I created and inhabited for all these years—how could I surrender them for the stairway's threat? As an officer in the air force I was instructed to adapt to all exigencies and adapt I will when the wobblies rear their ugly heads and try to tackle me.

I guess it all comes down to mind-set, how determined one is to battle the implacable transgressions of time. In the end, of course, time will triumph but, as I have found out, if it's in you, you can win a lot of skirmishes along the way, continuing to enjoy the journey.

My Uncle Lester is a good example of a skirmish survivor. Four months older than me (I won't go into that), Lester was an avid golfer who regularly won his club's senior championship trophy. But when he turned eighty he could no longer walk the eighteen holes (the club did not allow carts in the tournament) of the Rolling Hills Country Club to which he belonged. His shots were as strong as ever but navigating the terrain was too much for him.

Lester needed one more win, his twentieth, to retire the trophy and keep it permanently on his mantle, but it looked like he would not be able to compete. For weeks he brooded over being denied the chance to fulfill his dream of finally getting that trophy. His family and club members tried to console him.

Imagine their surprise when Lester showed up for the start of the senior tournament. He teed off, his customary long drive finding the middle of the fairway, but how would he get to the next tee at the top of the hill? A large burley man stepped forward, a professional wrestler, Iron Mike, whom Lester had hired to piggyback him around the course. The tournament officials searched the rulebook but could find nothing that prohibited this maneuver. Lester won by three strokes.

At the ceremony presenting him with the trophy, Lester announced that that was his last round of golf, and he gave his clubs to Iron Mike, who, sponsored by Lester, is now taking lessons from the club's pro.

QUERIES TO MY SEVENTIETH YEAR

Approaching, nearing, curious,
Thou dim, uncertain spectre—bringest thou life or
*   death?*
Strength, weakness, blindness, more paralysis and
*   heavier?*
Or placid skies and sun? Wilt stir the waters yet?
Or haply cut me short for good? Or leave me here as
*   now,*
Dull, parrot-like and old, with crack'd voice harping,
*   screeching?*

—Walt Whitman

The Past Is Sometimes
the Present

—

It is to be expected that as the years of old age go by, we seniors look less and less toward the retreating horizon, and more and more toward reminiscence—either the balmy sweet nostalgia of happy times or the bitter sorrow of regret, those missed opportunities and failed events that can sit heavily in one's chest like an insistent heartburn.

It is hard to imagine a recollected life that hasn't hoarded some joyful memories that can be reclaimed like treasure lifted from a buried chest. Perhaps there is an attic trunk that contains a random collection of letters filled with people and events, intimate moments, confessions, wisdom, disappointments, apologies, hope, disillusions, laughter, sorrow, all the emotions of life. For the nonagenarians who may be listing toward melancholia, in addition to these letters there probably are photographs and home movies of birthday parties, weddings, graduations, baptisms, bar mitzvahs and confirmations, school plays, ski trips, fishing moments, snowball fights, mortarboards and diploma handshakes, vacations here, there, and everywhere, new cars, Christmas trees, puppies, an 8mm of baby's first wobbly steps, initial attempts to roller skate, sleds toppling over in the snow, a succession of snowmen garlanded with knitted scarves; as I write this I am rummaging through my old keepsake box with its jumble of photos and countless spools of film that I'm sure will generate wonderful memories when I get around to viewing them.

Nostalgia may also be induced by the unearthing of long-neglected scrap books with all their preserved mementos: name tags, dance cards, report cards, invitations, announcements, newspaper notices, programs, menus, ticket stubs, itineraries, each encapsulated with pleasant recollections.

Comforting as nostalgia can be for those who look back upon the long years of their past with good humor, there are those who retrospectively find nothing but regret. "Youth is a blunder; manhood a struggle; old age a regret," Disraeli observed, and regret is indeed the bane of many seniors' retroactive passage through their earlier years. Instead of reveling in what was positive and successful and enlightening about his past, the regretter concentrates on what disappointed him. "The whole peninsula of Florida," Cynthia Ozick once pronounced in a sweeping generalization, "was weighted with regret. Everyone had left behind a real life."

Regret is often the bugaboo of elderly lives. Frequently it relates to failed romances and repudiated liaisons. How is a young man to know that his first true love will be the only real love of his life? In essence, that is the question that hangs over my old friend Hemingway's posthumous book, *A Moveable Feast*. He had three subsequent marriages but the final chapter, "There Is Never Any End to Paris," is a regretful love paean to Hadley, his first wife, whom he married when he was very young.

I myself have a regret related to Hemingway. In the winter of 1953 he invited me to join him and his wife, Mary, on an African safari he was going to write about for *Look* magazine. It was one of the last big game safaris. I did not go, for whatever reason I no longer remember, but later, when I read his essay in *Look,* replete with stunning photographs that showed me what I had missed, I was overcome with regret, as sharp today as it was back then. It is a regret I share with an elderly Henry James, who said: "I only regret in my chilled age certain occasions and possibilities I didn't embrace." As I have described in an earlier segment, later in my life I have gone on safaris, but Hemingway's was a major four-month old-fashioned safari that traveled from the banks of the Salengai to Tanganyika. I had fished and hunted with Ernest and accompanied him to many bullfights, steeplechase races, prizefights, and World Series games, but this safari would have topped them all and it remains a regret like no other.

Some reflections of regret are normal—how many old-sters have "embraced all occasions and possibilities," but obsessive regrets that turn into anger and rage can be self-destructive. As an example I have to look no further than my own father. To properly explain his rage, I have to go back to 1943 when I was an officer in the air force. I have previously referred to my being ordered to make a movie about the Antisubmarine Command despite my having never made a movie about anything. To edit the film, I had taken my raw footage to Hollywood where the First Motion Picture unit of the U.S. Air Force was located, hoping that by adding music and integrating the sound and titles they would be able to make a decent film out of it.

While there, I decided to try to find an Uncle Henry Hotchener I had never met, who had not dropped the middle "e" as my father had. Decimated by the Depression, my father was in awe of Uncle Henry who had been the business manager and confidante of the incomparable actor, John Barrymore, recently deceased. My father said that Barrymore had been totally dependent on Henry for all his business affairs and, in addition, that he wouldn't make a movie, or perform an important scene in that movie until my Aunt Marie, a Hollywood-famous astrologer, checked it out on her astrological charts.

Uncle Henry did not have a listed phone number so I went to his address, which was in an area north of Hollywood Boulevard, a section where there had been little development. It was an old unkempt house with weed-covered lawns and a decrepit driveway. The man who answered the door was dressed like a genie, a green genie, in a silk tunic and silk blousy pantaloons tapering into Arabian pointed, jeweled slippers, a wide-beaded and bejeweled belt around his waist, a huge gold scarab on a chain around his neck, and, incongruously, a tennis visor on his forehead. He looked at me, saying nothing. I started to explain who I was but he put a finger to his lips and gestured for me to follow him. The house was dimly lit and smelled of incense and musk. I followed him across the foyer and into what I supposed had been the dining room, but in the center of the room, in place of a dining table, there was an Indian funeral bier with a stout woman, shrouded in a flowing white gown, stretched out on it. Her hair and her complexion were as white as her gown. Her eyes were closed and her arms were crossed over her ample chest. A band of jewels encircled her forehead, and a scarab, identical to the one worn by my uncle, hung from a gold chain around her neck.

My uncle stopped at the bier and said, "Dear, this is Sam Hotchner's boy, now a lieutenant in the air force. This is my wife, Marie," he said, quite formally. I managed a "Pleased to meet you" but Aunt Marie did not move or reply. She wasn't dead, however, for I distinctly saw the rise and fall of her copious bosom. I guessed her to be a good twenty years older than my uncle. He led me into a butler's pantry where we sat on high stools while he spoke to me in a whisper, telling me that his wife had been so upset by Barrymore's death that she had been in a spiritual trance ever since.

Uncle Henry asked about my father but before I could answer we were both suddenly startled by a shrill sound that came from the dining room bier. My uncle immediately got off his stool and said I would have to be leaving. As we passed Aunt Marie she was droning a litany of strange sounds; a Hindu prayer for Barrymore's soul, my uncle explained.

At the door he gave me an embossed card with their names and address below, which was: "Theosophy & Abnormal Psychic Phenomena." "Tell your father," he said, "that we are developing this entire area. There's not much here now but after the war people will start to build and he can make his fortune. I've heard how bad things were for him and your family during the Depression, but this is his chance to recoup. We have building lots here for as little as a hundred dollars. Be sure tell him. I'd like to see you again while you are here, perhaps entertain you, but you see how things are . . ."

He quickly closed the door.

I wrote to my father about Henry's offer and enclosed his card, but my father's response was that he didn't put money in get-rich-quick schemes. Of course, my father had no money, but he did write to Uncle Henry and propose that he would buy a few lots if he could get them on credit, but he never received an answer from my uncle.

After the war, as my uncle had predicted, his area

suddenly flourished and the value of real estate soared. In the years that followed, my father occasionally berated his lost opportunity, but it wasn't until he turned eighty that his regret turned into an obsession, much of his anger directed at Uncle Henry who "with all his Barrymore money couldn't stake me to a couple of lousy lots. No, the poor relative out there in St. Louis, let him shift for himself. Would it have hurt him? Would it?"

In those Depression-heavy days, not yet lifted by the war, a hundred dollars was a considerable sum, and day after day, in his later years, my father excoriated Uncle Henry for causing him to miss that golden opportunity by not extending him credit, or, even worse, not answering his letter. On the day before he died from uremic poisoning, two days short of his eighty-fifth birthday, my father, half delirious, was still disjointedly railing against Uncle Henry, who had preceded him to the grave, and bemoaning the loss of the ephemeral Hollywood gold mine.

Those final years of his life, my father conformed to Dylan Thomas's exhortation that old age should burn and rage against the dying of the light.

There is a smoother course to follow on one's way to guidepost ninety-two and beyond, a course without rage that counterpoints Dylan's Welsh bombast, a course that I have tried to traverse, as described by Walter C. Hagen: "You're only here for a short visit. Don't hurry. Don't worry. And be sure to smell the flowers along the way."

Wherever your life ends, it is all there.
The advantage of living is not
measured by length, but by use;
some men have lived long, and lived little;
attend to it while you are in it. It lies in your will,
not in the number of years,
for you have lived enough.

—MONTAIGNE

You Are the Motorman,
Conductor, and Passenger

———

"Willpower" it is called, and it is an intrinsic asset all of us share to one degree or another. "Where there's a will there's a way" the old adage goes, and it speaks the truth. "Will" denotes a fixed or persistent intent or purpose, the power of one's mind to influence one's own actions, the dictionary says. Schopenhauer, who wrote the seminal work on the human will, identifies it as "a metaphysical existence that embellishes the actions of individuals."

For super seniors whose strengths are waning, calling on their will may activate a reserve of strength and purpose. No better example can be found than how the ninety-year-old John Adams, the second president of the United States, and eighty-three-year-old Thomas Jefferson, the third president, simultaneously exerted their willpower in July of 1826 to defy their imminent deaths.

Both men, along with Benjamin Franklin, had drafted

the Declaration of Independence, but their friendship had frayed over serious political disagreements during George Washington's presidency. In 1789, Adams was elected president with the highest number of electoral votes, and Jefferson, who had the second highest, despite their animosity, automatically became vice president, the procedure at that time. The two men were at loggerheads all during Adams's presidency.

In the next election they opposed each other, the president running against his vice president. Their dislike for each other resulted in the first mud-slinging campaign in the history of American politics. Jefferson's spokesmen maintained that President Adams had "a hideous hermaphroditical character, which has neither the force and firmness of a man, nor the gentleness and sensibility of a woman."

Adams's people responded in kind, calling Jefferson "the son of a half-breed Indian squaw, sired by a Virginia mulatto father." In the crescendo of the dirty campaign, Adams was attacked as "a fool, a hypocrite, a criminal, and a tyrant," and Jefferson, in turn, was called "a weakling, an atheist, a libertine, and a coward." The venom was infectious, the papers quoting Martha Washington as denouncing Jefferson as "one of the most detestable of mankind." It was as a result of this vicious infighting that an allegation took hold that Jefferson had lived with one of his slaves, Sally Hemmings, with whom he sired five children.

Jefferson won the election but at the end of his two-term

presidency he characterized those years as "splendid misery," Adams had retreated into a satisfactory retirement and Jefferson was also pleased to retire to his beloved Monticello. With their political passions cooled, the two men were able to restore the deep friendship they had shared all during the Revolutionary years.

Toward the end of June, 1826, both men had fallen seriously ill, and on July 1st their respective doctors pronounced them on the verge of death and their families were summoned to their bedsides. But Adams and Jefferson had made a solemn pact that they would stay alive until July Fourth, the fiftieth anniversary of that day they had created with their remarkable document. Each day their doctors predicted their deaths by nightfall but each day the two men sustained their allegiance to their vow, inquiring whether the other was holding on.

On the afternoon of July Fourth, hearing the sounds of celebration outside their windows, these two old patriots honored their commitments to each other and died within a few hours of each other, shrouded in the glory of the day they had helped to create.

True willpower, as exemplified in that extraordinary feat of the dying ex-presidents, exists apart from ambition, which is an overall desire for success, power, wealth, and the like, a desire that motivates us to get ahead, go up the social ladder, get our name on the door. But it is not aimed at a specific target as the will is. "You can do what you will,"

Schopenhauer said, "but in any given moment of your life, you can *will* only one definite thing and absolutely nothing other than that one thing." In other words, the exercise of our will is an obsession that drives us to a specific goal, brooking no distractions. It exists in all of us, although infrequently summoned.

In my life, I have relied on the tenacity of my will several times, beginning when I was twelve years old. The Depression had battered our family, rendering us penniless and reduced to living in one room in a sleazy hotel. It was summer, a St. Louis summer where the heat rivaled equatorial Africa. My brother had been farmed out to relatives in Keokuk, Iowa, for a dollar a week; my mother, ill with tuberculosis, was confined in the Fee-Fee Sanitarium on the outskirts of the city; my father was traveling throughout Missouri, Kansas, and Oklahoma, fruitlessly trying to sell watches to people who didn't have money for food, let alone watches.

We were seriously in arrears with our twenty-seven dollars a month rent, and an Innkeeper's Eviction Notice had been taped to our door as it had been to most of the doors in the Westgate Hotel. I had pleaded with the hotel owner, Mr. Todes, putting on my best poor little boy all alone performance, but he said the bank had now foreclosed on the hotel and banks didn't deal with twelve-year-old boys. I knew that Ben, the sadistic bellhop, was ready to slap his big Yale lock on our door as soon as the room was unoccupied, and confiscate everything in it, but the law held him at bay as long as I occupied the room.

I ripped that eviction notice off the door, double-locked it from the inside, and vowed, with all my will, not to budge from our room, thereby protecting our belongings.

Those belongings consisted of our canary, Skippy, and his cage, our four threadbare overcoats (St. Louis was as cold in the winter as it was hot in the summer), two pairs of galoshes, a pile of outdated *Woman's Home Companion*s, an Atwater Kent Radio with burned-out tubes, a single-shaft umbrella with a bone handle that had been given to my father by his father when he left Kraków, several patched sweaters, my one twisted necktie, an illegal one-burner electric grill, a bag full of marbles I had won, my prized collection of rare cigar bands, my brother's red scooter, a pair of Keds with the rubber name tag hanging loose, my mother's hand mirror, and a radio crystal box I had made in school. It may not seem like a collection that merited my devotion but it was all we had in the world and there was no way that that repulsive Ben was going to get his hands on any of it, particularly Skippy, whom he threatened to feed to his equally repulsive cat as soon as he could get his hands on him.

What little food I had soon ran out. The hotel cut off our electricity, disconnected the room phone, and did what they could to make my life miserable. I saved a box of bread crumbs for Skippy but in time my hunger made me so desperate I resorted to cutting out luscious food ads from one of the *Woman's Home Companions* and eating them. It was amazing how, as I chewed on a brightly colored roast beef, my imagination made it actually taste like roast beef. I also kept myself filled to the top with water.

Ben banged on the door several times every day and night during these weeks, and barked ominous threats, but despite my terror, my resolve stayed firm: I would not, *would not,* surrender that room.

How it ended, there was a faint knock on the door, obviously not Ben's. I climbed up on top of a table and looked out the open transom. Standing there was my little brother, holding his cardboard suitcase. My Keokuk relatives had sent him back on the bus because, despite being warned repeatedly, my father had failed to pay his one-dollar indenture. But my father redeemed himself by hurrying back to St. Louis and renting a two-room apartment from a landlord so desperate for tenants he conceded the first two months rent.

That early triumph of my will ingrained in me confidence for what I could overcome with willpower, and I relied on it at critical moments in my life. I know that a strong will is in all of us, a ready ally, all you need is the courage and strength to let it fight your battles with you.

At no time is a strong, positive will more needed than when an elderly person is faced with a diagnosis of a potentially fatal disease, such as cancer. There is research that demonstrates how two patients of similar ages, with the same diagnosis, undergoing the same treatment, often develop opposite results. The defining factor: One patient was optimistic and determined about his chances of recovery, the other pessimistic, giving up and regarding his diagnosis as a death sentence.

Oncology physicians now often incorporate mental techniques such as meditation, biofeedback, and visualization (creating in the mind positive images about what is occurring in the body). According to the prestigious oncology doctors, E. H. and I. R. Rosenbaum, physicians believe that a patient's positive attitude may even have a direct effect on cell function and consequently may be used to arrest, if not cure the patient's cancer. They emphasize the advantage patients have who decide, after the initial shock of being told the bad news wears off, that they will stand up and fight the disease, continuing to get as much out of their daily lives as they can. Recent research has found that these positive patients trigger a spot in the brain that excretes a fluid that actually combats the cancer cells.

When Stanley, a feisty eighty-one, found out he had cancer, his doctor told him that the best way he could help himself was by being aggressive, "Stand up and fight it," the doctor said.

Stanley took his advice literally and enrolled in his YMCA's boxing program for seniors. Along with his chemo treatment, Stanley occasionally punched the bag, skipped rope, shadowboxed and, in the ring, practiced punching his gloves into his instructor's padded hand targets.

Of course, Stanley never actually fought anyone, and there were days when he couldn't make the gym, but the doctors said that his determination to keep to his boxing routine despite the chemo's assault on him, was a strong factor in his eventual recovery.

I have often observed the beneficial effect of a positive attitude toward combating cancer. Twenty years ago, along with Paul Newman, I helped start a camp for children with cancer, the Hole in the Wall Gang Camp in Ashford, Connecticut. I have seen children arrive at camp depressed and withdrawn, not communicating, who were completely changed by the positive attitude instilled in them by the pervasive optimism that emanates from the nurses, doctors, counselors, and from other campers who, with similar cancers, are determinedly aggressive toward their condition. There's little doubt that the change in these new arrivals was attributable to the optimistic support that surrounded them, particularly those other children in their group who were not letting their affliction get them down.

Oncology doctors who spent time at the camp found that positive support works as well for adults as it does for these children. There are seniors who react to a cancer diagnosis by retreating into being alone and preparing for death, thereby cutting themselves off from the possibility of achieving remission. But those, like Stanley, who continue to interact with friends and family and take advantage of support programs, group therapy, and counseling have a much better chance of survival.

Now, shifting to the sublime, there is my dear friend, Florence Olian, who just turned ninety-seven. She lives in California and when she was ninety-three, she wrote this log of her life as she saw it on her way to one hundred:

HOW I'M GOING TO MAKE IT TO ONE HUNDRED

When I was 15, I only wanted to make it to age 16
so I could get my driver's license.
When I was 20 I could not wait to vote
for the President (FDR) for the first time.
The years have passed.
I found the love of my life and marriage
was a great adventure.
Then motherhood was the crowning
moment of my life.
Time races on.
Children are grown and gone.
My husband is, too. We had so much fun
as senior citizens seeing the world.

Now I live alone but never stop learning.
Every morning I see the sunrise over
the mountains.
Celebrating my 90th birthday was
unforgettable.
I am accepting every wrinkle.
I have seen Mount Kilimanjaro.
And I can still read without glasses.
I like barbecued ribs, a glass of good
wine and listening to opera.
I am 93 and hope to—no, make that,
will *reach 100.*
I have found that a sense of humor
and positive attitude keep all the
sad memories and regrets pushed out
of my mind without guilt.
And I say,
"Florence, live the moment."

NO FUNERAL GLOOM

No funeral gloom, my dears, when I am gone,
corpse-gazing, tears, black raiment, graveyard
  grimness.
Think of me as withdrawn into dimness.
yours still, you mine.
Remember all the best
Of our past moments,
and forget the rest,
and so, to where I wait, come gently on.
                    —*William Allingham*

The Train Is Pulling Out, Step Gently On

———

You had no say about your entrance upon life's stage but now you are the star, director, and producer of the last act's finale. You can glide softly into the wings, without curtain speech or fanfare, or you can light up the stage for your final curtain. The beauty of this performance, if you choose to stage it, is that you have a captive audience and no critics in attendance.

There are those who wish to have nothing to do with plans for their departure, not caring a fig what happens after the lights go down. But, then again, there are others who want to micromanage their departure, from casket to resting place, eulogists to flower arrangements, music to post-funeral refreshments, shivas and wakes to obituaries.

A woman I know, poised for her finale, has engaged a prominent mezzo-soprano to sing her favorite operatic aria, and there's an elderly fellow in Armonk who has contracted a jazz trio to ensure that his "event" won't be somber but a lively toe-tapping celebration of his life.

Some nonagenarians actually want to participate in their funeral proceedings. They have recorded speeches that will be played in the funeral home or church; others have gone a step further and videotaped themselves talking to the mourners on a screen above the casket. On the dark side, there are deceases-to-be who have named certain people they do not want at their funerals. I suppose the ones who are videotaping themselves could work in a few malicious things to say about their enemies, perhaps their nasty landlords or their ex-wives or ex-husbands who, they assure the mourners, shortened their lives. It's a great opportunity to even the score with anyone who has rubbed the deceased the wrong way. No need to worry—they can't sue for libel.

While we're on the subject of the videotapers, I suggest they have it done properly by professionals who provide makeup, teleprompters, lighting, and staging; otherwise, if the super senior does it himself, it will be badly lighted, badly focused, and badly performed. You don't want your last image on earth to make you look like Willie Werewolf or Malaria Mary.

So for your farewell video I think you should imagine you are getting an Academy Award for lifetime achievement, and, in time-honored Oscar tradition, you can pull a paper out of your pocket and read a list of thank-yous, all the people who have contributed something to your life. If you have the moxie for it, you might even thank the mother of your illegitimate child.

Another suggestion: You should concentrate on writing the punch line for your tombstone; a bell-ringing zinger might get posted on the Internet and put you on the road to immortality. You may want to invest in a professional writer who might come up with a tombstone original that would score in this crowded genre.

You do not have to feel self-conscious about enumerating the things you'd like to have accompany you in your casket. King Tut did it, why not you? Although your cousin Harry may have often voiced his admiration for your vintage Cartier's wristwatch, you should not let that deter you if you'd like to have it on your wrist when you go down under. Same goes for younger sister Hazel's envy of your set of filigreed garnet necklace and matching bracelet, which you plan to wear at your viewing.

Despite these anomalies, most elderlies do not concern themselves with the aftermath of their departures. Or the departure itself. The ones who are able to stay busy concentrate on their endeavors, giving little or no thought to the end of a life that still has meaning and vitality for them. I am one of those, too occupied to give much thought to the Great Beyond. I have no truck with heaven or reincarnation, but I do have faith in the endurance of my soul, a faith that originated in Soldan High School when the reading assignment in my American Literature class was a short story of Ernest Hemingway's entitled, "Now I Lay Me" that began:

> I myself did not want to sleep because I had been living for a long time with the knowledge that if I ever shut my eyes in the dark and let myself go, my soul would go out of my body. I had been that way for a long time, ever since I had been blown up at night and felt it go out of me and go off and then come back. I tried never to think about it, but it had started to go since in the nights, just at the moment of going off to sleep, and I could only stop it by a very great effort. So while now I am fairly sure that it would not really have gone out, yet then, that summer, I was unwilling to make the experiment.

I was startled by this concept of an active soul, so vital to the existence of the narrator (obviously autobiographical) of the story. The crunch of the Depression had suppressed our family's religious beliefs but if such a soul existed inside of me then perhaps I could believe in that (I was fourteen years old at the time).

We had to write an essay about the story, and to overcome my usual skepticism about ephemeral matters, I applied myself assiduously to researching the soul.

I began with my *Webster's* dictionary: "soul *n* the principle of life, feeling, thought, and action in humans, regarded as a distinct entity separate from the body, the spiritual part of humans as distinct from the physical."

This certainly was an intriguing overture that motivated me to intensify my research. I consulted a professor who taught theology, the campus chaplain, the rabbi of Temple Israel, the adviser of the campus Catholic Club. In the library I found persuasive quotes:

PLATO: The soul of man is immortal and imperishable.

THOMAS BISHOP: John Brown's body lies a-mouldering in the grave. His soul goes marching on!

WORDSWORTH: Milton!... Thy soul was like a Star, and dwelt apart.

SOCRATES: Either death is a state of nothingness and utter unconsciousness, or, as men say, there is a change and migration of the soul from this world to another.

I received an A+ on my essay and I was on my way to believing in the existence of my soul.

A year later, my belief was bolstered when, as an assignment in my advanced Latin class, I read Cicero's disquisition on old age, *De Senectute,* which contains a deeply persuasive account of the nature and importance of his soul.

Later in life, when I became friends with Ernest, I told

him how his story had impacted me, and one evening in Venice, over a bottle of Valpolicella, he spoke at length about the propensities and mysticism of his soul. He had just survived a near-death experience in Africa when a de Havilland airplane, attempting to rescue him and his wife, Mary, from the jungle, crashed on takeoff. So he was feeling very intimate with his soul, which, he said, had been on alert.

Over the years, I have silently communicated with the souls of some of the people who had been part of my life. By this I don't mean recalling specific events or adventures with them—I do cherish those memories—but I actually connect with them at certain times when they appear and give me support and encouragement, sympathy and intimate humor, and I see them as clearly as the last time I saw them.

And I believe that when the time comes for departure, my soul, immortal and imperishable, will hang around to perpetuate who I was, what I did, and the love I emanated. But for now, my soul is snug in my hospitable body, which serves me well despite a few inevitable nicks and dents.

> *My abs have gone to flabs,*
> *My belly's turned to jelly,*
> *My brain has a strain down its grain.*
> *But my luck she is a-holdin'*

And my love life still is golden,
And that's my nonagenarian refrain.

I live my life now as I have always lived it. I have lost close friends and family but I rejoice in the friends and family that I do have. I go where I've always gone, do what I've always done, along with my incandescent wife who illuminates my everyday life, and my remarkable children who pal around with me, sharing our affections. It's nice that both my son Timothy and stepson Alex are following in my footsteps, O.J. in the morning, gin and tonic at night.

In the central place of every heart there is a recording chamber; so long as it receives messages of beauty, hope, cheer and courage, so long are you young. When the wires are all down and your heart is covered with the snows of pessimism and the ice of cynicism, then, and then only are you grown old.

—GEN. DOUGLAS MACARTHUR

By the Light of the
Lopsided Moon

~

I had a dream last night. I am riding along a highway in my '61 Corvette convertible. I am enjoying the warm, seductive night air that is washing over my face, and the low-lying stars reaching down to me. I have never been happier. We have the highway to ourselves, Vette and I, nothing else moving, this direction or that.

A red light pops up on the dashboard where the fuel gauge shows empty. I turn the Vette off the highway onto a path that leads to a field awash in flowers, yellow in the light of the lopsided moon. The engine sighs and gently expires. There is silence now, except for the sad call of a mourning dove in the distance.

Over the years, Vette and I have traveled to many good places: the low bridge over Lake Pontchartrain; the causeway to Key West; the violent lightning storms on the high passes of the Poconos; the mountainous route to Ensenada;

the roads of the Sawtooth Mountain; along the Atlantic, New York to Cape Cod. You do not show your age, Vette, but I show mine.

I hang my cap on the rearview mirror, lean back and rest the back of my head on the supple leather of my seat. Looking up at the sky, I see that the stars have not followed us from the highway and the moon has suddenly turned as yellow as the flowers. I try to speak to the moon but I have nothing to say. The mourning dove continues to broadcast its plaintive coo. I close my eyes, put my cap over my face, and await the dawn.

Acknowledgments

My friend Florence Olian for "How I'm Going to Make It to One Hundred."

Virginia Kiser Hotchner for suggesting the title and much more.

Claire Panke and Anna Harding for their painstaking assistance.

Tracy and Holly Hotchner for bringing Ernie into my life.

Dr. Norman Kelman, in memorium.

Washington University Alumni Office

Andrew Padula, former V.P. for Production, Bigelow Tea Co., for his recollections.

Kathryn Huck for making the demands of editing this book a piece of St. Martin's cake.